Living ... nt

Living With Unemployment

ANN WARREN

HODDER AND STOUGHTON
LONDON   SYDNEY   AUCKLAND   TORONTO

British Library Cataloguing in Publication Data

Warren, Ann
 Living with unemployment.
 1. Unemployment — Great Britain —
 Religious aspects — Christianity
 2. Adjustment (Psychology)
 I. Title
 261.8'5   BR115.E3

ISBN 0-340-40125-7

Copyright © 1986 by Ann Warren. First printed 1986. All rights reserved. No part of this publication may be reproduced or transmitted in any form or by any means, electronic or mechanical, including photocopy, recording, or any information storage and retrieval system, without permission in writing from the publisher. Printed in Great Britain for Hodder and Stoughton Limited, Mill Road, Dunton Green, Sevenoaks, Kent by Hunt Barnard Printing Ltd., Aylesbury, Bucks.

Hodder and Stoughton Editorial Office: 47 Bedford Square, London WC1B 3DP

For

Simon and Angie,
Tim and Jill,
Chris and Ann

and many other friends around the country who have shared their experiences for the help of readers, and in particular for the people of Comex and other friends in the Walsall area.

Contents

	Foreword	9
1	When Unemployment Strikes	11
2	A Real Bereavement Experience	19
3	Who I Am or What I Do	27
4	Things Ain't What They Used to Be	35
5	Time on Your Hands	43
6	The Support Group	49
7	New Beginnings	57
8	For the Wife	65
9	Role Swapping, or Who Pays the Bills?	71
10	Unemployment – What Can We Do to Help?	75
11	Money, Greed and All That	81
12	'Unemployment for the Christian or A Way that You May be Able to Bear It'	89
13	A Christian View of Work and the Future	99

Foreword

I was asked by a friend to write this book in the very first week that Peter was out of work, and I know now the reason for the request.

When people are actually faced with the downtime of unemployment it can be so very difficult to know where to begin to look for help. Moreover, since others in the same situation hardly ever talk about what they are going through, we are often left with the impression that all these bitter hurts and feelings of rejection are ours alone – or that no one else could possibly understand.

Rereading some of the experiences that we and others have shared brings back painful memories that all of us would much rather forget. But for the sake of those going through the unemployment jungle today, I have felt it right to leave the experiences on paper as they are, in the hope that they might be of some help to readers in the same situation.

During the course of my research for the book I have talked to people in all walks of life and in every age group, but inevitably I have written more about unemployment in the executive and professional categories since this is our own personal background. Many of the experiences are in any case the *same* for *everyone*, wherever they come from, and once you have been unemployed you learn to speak a common language which is the same wherever you go.

The problem is vast, covering much more than the tip of the iceberg that most people see, and no single book could possibly do justice to the subject. My prayer is simply that what I have written may be of some help to those at present out of work, and others who long to help and stand by their friends at such a time.

1

When Unemployment Strikes

A Day Like Any Other

It was a workday evening like any other – 6.30 p.m. in the usual rush of getting supper ready, chasing the children to finish off their homework, and wondering whether the train bringing my husband home from London would be late yet again.

And then as he walked in the door I saw the look on his face and stopped dead in my tracks.

'Is anything wrong?' I heard myself ask, without really needing to know the answer.

His voice sounded taut and unreal as he automatically began putting things away for the sake of something to do.

'I've just been told that I am being made redundant,' he said, and in those few words a great shadow seemed to fall across our little world, making everything darker and more uncertain than we should ever have believed possible.

They say that you always know when this kind of news is in the offing, and that the writing is on the wall for those who want to read it – but at this particular moment in time we were both surprisingly unprepared.

About eighteen months earlier the happy thriving company that Peter worked for had been taken over in a dawn raid on the Stock Exchange. The circumstances surrounding the bid were such that the rules were immediately changed so that a 'takeover' like that could never happen again to any other company. But frankly this was little consolation, and we could only ask, numbly, 'Why did God allow this to happen to us?'

One by one my husband's colleagues left or were pushed out, and parts of the company that they had all worked so hard to build up were sold or poised ready under the axe. The head office was moved from the small cosy riverside building where everyone knew everyone else to a large, ugly Victorian edifice with anonymous glass doors along an echoing corridor, where no one seemed to belong or feel wanted.

At the time we agonised over what was the right thing to do. All our instincts were for Peter to get out and leave the new owners to it. They had borrowed millions of pounds to buy the company, and brought nothing in return, except the most colossal overdraft.

In any climate other than a roaring recession where there were simply no jobs to go to, most people would probably have left anyway. But our own particular dilemma had another horn to it. Because this was originally an old family company Peter felt it right to stay on and try to salvage something of what little remained. The many hundreds of people he had worked with on estates on the other side of the world needed to know that there was still someone at the centre who cared – and indeed a number of them had personally begged him not to leave. We had no guidance to go, and so we stayed.

But the following year was an agonising and disheartening experience, watching the company going steadily downhill and further and further into the red. Peter was still 'there' but powerless to help as he was forced to stand by and watch the assets of our old company being sold off one by one to fund their borrowings for the takeover. The daily work that had been so challenging and enjoyable, as he had helped to build it up and watched it grow, now became a depressing grind. He went through the motions, but the challenge had gone and only drudgery remained.

When the year was up things seemed almost at rock bottom so that there was no other way out, but then as the new owners sold off a couple more precious assets we surveyed the wreckage. Was it possible ever to recover and build up again on what was left?

Peter felt that the bottom had been reached and that the future could only be better. He kept doggedly on in the belief that at least his part of the company still looked good and would continue to receive support. Ironically he had almost stopped worrying when the bank called in more of its loan for the takeover, and his corner of the company was sold as well...

It is difficult to describe what happens to you when unemployment strikes. There is so much more involved than most people ever even think about.

For a start it could hardly have come at a worse time in our lives. Two of our three children were just coming up to crucial exams in local schools. Elderly relations on both sides of the family were very much in need of help and support and at the same time, humanly speaking, our best hopes of employment lay on the other side of the earth, or in some other remote corner of the globe. Twenty years of experience in managing tropical agriculture and overseas trading was hardly the ideal qualification for a secure local job, especially in a recession like this.

Frantic plans rushed through our minds, and probably in those first few weeks our actions bore more resemblance to those of drowning swimmers than trusting Christians.

As so many others do, Peter took his redundancy as a personal rejection – and since he already suffered from a deep but well-hidden lack of confidence in his own ability, this only served to make the whole situation worse. He was secretly convinced that no one would ever want either him or his services again, and the more he heard about others out of work and the millions joining the dole queue the more this fear seemed to assume the shape of reality.

For myself the impact was very different and I could not at the time have put words to my feelings. Something deep inside me seemed to have snapped and I found myself going off quietly to have a good cry more often than I care to admit. The pain was very deep and I could not at first get to grips with what was happening to me.

On the surface was the whole panic situation of our home and family. Where were we to go? Should we really have to pack up and travel to some remote corner of the earth just at a time when the children needed us around so much? And, on the other hand, how could we drag them away from their friends in the local church and from all that they had come to love about their home surroundings at this most vulnerable time in their lives?

I was vividly reminded of a story one of my colleagues on our late-night television show *Company* had told me just a few weeks before. It was about a family who had all their belongings stacked outside their house on a barrow because they were being evicted. An old lady passing by had looked down kindly at the little girl clutching her canary in a cage, and said, 'Poor child, I am so sorry you've lost your home.'

Without a moment's hesitation the little girl replied, 'Oh no, we've still got our home, but at the moment we've nowhere to put it.'

At the time that story had brought tears to my eyes because it spoke to me so much of my own early childhood. But now it seemed to have a much deeper significance.

WHEN UNEMPLOYMENT STRIKES

A very large part of the trouble for me was the knowledge that we had 'a home', but might well have nowhere to put it – that almost any change would involve some kind of 'home destruction'. The very roots of our most vital relationships were being shaken, and my own bereavement experiences were telling me that I really could not go through all this *again*.

If the truth were told, I was finding it difficult if not impossible really to trust God in this situation. Years ago when I was only 7 my world had fallen apart in what seemed to be alarmingly similar circumstances. My mother and father had taken me out of London during the blitz to live in rented accommodation in Cambridge. Because my father could not get a reasonable job there my mother had to work as well, so that I hardly ever saw them. And then within two years they had both died, leaving me alone in the local convent to face what turned out to be an even more uncertain future...

I had only recently come to the point where I could accept that God had 'allowed' some of these early traumas to happen to me for a reason, and now it seemed that He was asking me to trust Him all over again with the future and safety of our own children – to accept that whatever the situation appeared to be, He still knew best. Frankly I was finding that kind of trust a pretty impossible exercise!

Everything around us seemed to militate against this trust. Unemployment around the world was reaching epidemic proportions, with well over three million out of work in this country alone. Two hundred people were currently applying for every job for which Peter was qualified. And two of his Christian friends with similar experience and abilities were still out of work after over a year of searching. Indeed, in some areas thousands seemed almost permanently in the dole queues. The future looked very bleak indeed.

For Peter, trusting God involved a very different

exercise. Whatever other problems he had known, there had always been enough money and somewhere to live, and he had worked in the same company for twenty years without a break. Ironically this was now proving almost more of a problem to him than my fears and feelings were to me.

The very fact that he had not had to go looking for a job for many years meant that he had no way of proving his own ability to himself, or for that matter of seeing how valuable his gifts might be to other people.

The coming months were obviously going to be a make-or-break experience, but it was not a happy prospect for any of us.

Over and over again during the time that Peter was out of work we saw that God promises to help us *in* the situation, rather than to protect us *from* it. So many Christians seem to look on their faith as some sort of insurance policy against physical or material hardship. But one of my favourite verses has always been, 'No temptation has overtaken you that is not common to man. God is faithful, and he will not let you be tempted beyond your strength, but...will also provide the way of escape, that you may be able to endure it' (I Cor. 10:13).

Just like anyone else, we should have loved God to reach down and rescue us from the situation, but I personally believe that looking at our faith in this way is very simplistic and profoundly unhelpful to those around us.

The fact is that millions of people around the world are going through the same hardships, often with a great deal less help and security than we ourselves have known. Many have little hope of any employment in the foreseeable future. Indeed there are some in the inner-city areas of places like Liverpool where permanent unemployment is entering the second generation of families, with a degree of hopelessness largely unknown in Western society.

Sociologists assure us that some degree of unemployment is not only here to stay, but is on the increase. So it seems only honest to look at what this feels like 'from the inside', and at the many ways in which God helped us actually *in* the situation, rather than endlessly discussing political solutions to the problem, and ways to prevent it – desirable and necessary as these undoubtedly are.

During our time out of work we have learnt a great deal about people and things that help us most, and about those that frankly do not! We have discovered how much help there is available on a practical level – if you know where to go. And by this I mean really useful down-to-earth help in assessing one's abilities and job prospects – help that is often not available to those who need it most.

This book is intended to spread such help around a little, and to share our experiences with those who are in the same plight, as well as with those who long to help and who understand what it feels like to be unemployed.

2

A Real Bereavement Experience

Being unemployed is like having the toothache – it never leaves you alone day or night. When you wake up in the morning it is there worrying away at you in the stillness: in the early hours it faces you with nothing but uncertainty and an empty day ahead. And all the time the consequences are obvious and all pervading.

When unemployment had not happened to *us*, but was only something that 'they' experienced, I used to think of it only in terms of financial deprivation – not having enough to pay the gas bill or the mortgage. I certainly hadn't the least idea of how far reaching the consequences could be.

What goes on in our lives at this time has an almost total fall-out effect, in our homes, our relationships, our everyday activities, and all the little things that we had never realised were so important. Just about everything comes under fire and it is good to be ready for this.

After many years of a really pressurised, commuter life style, working out of the country for between three and four months a year, Peter's first reaction after the shock of it all was to collapse into the welcoming arms of his own home. No need to prise himself out of bed to the demanding buzz of an alarm-clock every morning; plenty of time to potter around the house and do all the things he had always meant to do. But was it really like that?

In a very short time the welcome break had a distinctly hollow ring to it, and many other more sinister pressures began to creep in. The realisation that this interval could well be permanent began to hit home.

A man's working life so fills most of his day that suddenly to remove this from him is little short of a bereavement experience. So said John, a senior executive who had been fired at twenty-four-hours' notice in the middle of a successful career.

The experience is as close and traumatic as losing a loved one by death or divorce. I still do not know the cause, and the trauma was therefore compounded because no one could give me a reason. Profits were good and I hadn't stolen anything – indeed they seem to have valued my services enough to give me a five-year contract only three months earlier. The chairman merely stated that he had made a mistake and I had lost the confidence of the board. The sense of pain was therefore acute because it was so sudden. There was a deep sense of betrayal, and in addition I had a terrible feeling of rejection and isolation which I suppose it is impossible for anyone to understand who has not experienced this trauma.

On one day you are consulted, decisions have to be taken and you are, like the centurion, telling people to come and they come, to go and they go. The next day you have nothing. What is the point of getting out of bed? What does your family, and especially your wife think of you?

Your friends express horror and surprise, but like a dread disease or death you can see their eyes flicker away and their thoughts express themselves silently. 'Oh Lord, how embarrassing. I don't really want to be involved.'

Everyday Things

The most devastating ongoing effect will probably be the loss of things we have never even thought seriously about before – travelling to or from the office or the factory, the people we have worked with, the ordinary everyday things that we have done for years.

Technically, theoretically, there is probably no reason why we should not go on seeing these people, but somehow it is never quite the same. We no longer belong to or fit in as part of the scene.

One man in the Midlands told me he had lost sight of all his mates at the factory where he had worked for fifteen years. The only news he had of them now was the occasional notice of a death in the papers.

Another one who had been out of work for over a year was quite blunt about it. 'You can have absolutely no idea of how much I miss my work,' he said. 'Just the companionship and the ongoing interest of working together to achieve a common goal. I'll never get over this, and in my view nothing can replace this for me.'

The personal impact for us was different. Most of Peter's work had been with people on the other side of the world, and there seemed no reason and no possibility of ever going back to visit the many familiar people and places that had deeply involved us.

For the previous few years I had been editor of the world-wide company magazine, and the managing director had once commented that I knew more people and more about the company than almost anyone else. The sense of bereavement for me was therefore much stronger than for most wives in this position – but it was not *my* life's work.

Putting the Past Behind Us

When I first told our friend Edward England about Peter's redundancy, he said, 'New things are only possible when old things come to an end.' Of course he was absolutely right, but I'm not sure that either of us wanted to hear that at the time.

It was quite a while before Peter was really able to put the past behind him, and he seemed to find it almost impossible to look in any other direction. He had been doing the job he wanted to do, he and his colleagues had built up the group together step by step. What on earth was the point of starting all over again at 49 – even if he could – just to have someone else put the axe to his work a few years later?

As in any bereavement it may take time to work out some of the negative emotions that are churning around inside us before we can begin to move forward to whatever lies ahead with any kind of positive feeling. In fact, it will be quite impossible to think creatively about the future until we have got rid of such feelings once and for all.

Coping with the Black Side of Unemployment

Everyone spoke of the same two emotions in the early days of redundancy – first, a numbing sense of shock and unreality. 'Surely this can't really be happening to me – there must be some mistake?' And then anger.

The twilight zone when redundancy hits is very similar to that of the bereaved person unable to face up to the loss of a loved one. There is a very natural clinging to what has been, and a total inability to face up to what has to be done.

It is not uncommon to feel as if one has received a body blow physically, shrinking in self-esteem and the ability to enjoy life. Many people speak of loss of appetite, both physical and sexual, and a total sense of lethargy and depression with no energy left for ordinary everyday things.

Just as in bereavement, these feelings have got to be dealt with and 'let out' or they will cause havoc in the mind and the body. If they are not, the consequences are inevitable and we enter a permanent state of hopelessness and despair.

A doctor has stated, in the *British Medical Journal* that 'The gloom and depression emanating from such people are as contagious as tuberculosis and about as dangerous, causing severe effects in the families of the unemployed.'

The more resilient and naturally self-confident people will probably not remain in this state very long. As the initial shock wears off they will quickly become angry about all that has happened to them.

Chris had been presented with an ultimatum by the company he had worked with for seventeen years: either take on an appointment thousands of miles away in Zaire, or accept inevitable redundancy. The post would have meant splitting up their very close family of five children – the youngest still a baby – and so he chose to stay.

'My reaction was a very normal and healthy one,' he says. Passing quickly from disbelief – 'Surely they can't really mean *me*?' and 'Something is bound to come up' – to some quite heavy anger on the subject. 'Why *me*, and after all those years of faithful work! How unfair!'

Fortunately for Chris, he had already seen what happened to people who did not work their way through the normal psychological processes of redundancy. Somehow they never emerged from their original state of bewilderment and shock, remaining paralysed by all that had happened to them. As he rightly realised, these people really needed help in working out their feelings and letting out the anger that was seething down there somewhere.

Depression itself is often a result of not giving vent to

one's feelings, and can be diagnosed as nothing more than repressed anger. Sitting under a heap of negative emotions that have never been allowed to see the light of day is enough to kill all hopes and positive thinking about the future.

Everyone needs someone to talk to – and if necessary to shout at – about what has happened. Many people feel that they cannot talk to their wives or their friends about this, but this kind of depression is self-feeding. *Everyone* needs to talk it out in reasonable depth.

Being stuck in the dole queues week after week is a perfect recipe for despair, especially in those areas where factories and workshops have closed down for good without any prospect of new businesses moving in. It is too easy for people in this situation to hide away at home feeling that the whole situation is hopeless. Above all they need someone to get them out of themselves and make them realise that they still have some value in the world.

Whatever the unemployment situation you are facing and whatever the job prospects may be, it is vital to get rid of any bitter, destructive emotions and to put the past behind you.

Continually nursing anger and bitterness inside yourself about what has happened will almost certainly hurt you more than anyone. Certainly it will have no effect on the people towards whom it is directed, and brooding on the situation will soak most of your energies into the downward spiral of despair, preventing you from moving out into the future *whatever* that may hold.

Forgiveness the Only Way

After a number of weeks, passing through shock and anger about his sudden dismissal, John said, 'I came to realise that all the anger and bitterness that I was experiencing would not get me my job back. Forgiveness of those who had treated me in this way was the only possible route forward.'

Needless to say this is difficult if not impossible without allowing the grace of God to work in us, as Chris's wife found out:

> For a while I thought it must all be a mistake – surely it couldn't be my husband that they meant to get rid of? As the full realisation dawned I became deeply angry because I felt that the redundancy was a personal slight on his character and performance. This anger was something I was quite unable to come to terms with until I became a Christian.

Peter had worked through much of his anger and frustration during the weeks following the takeover, and had eventually found the grace to forgive those responsible – something, incidentally, that some of his non-Christian colleagues found quite hard to stomach. But now that he and so many others were being made redundant it was *my* turn.

I was furious that a quick night raid on the Stock Exchange could effectively destroy the livelihood of so many people just for the gain of a few.

All those involved, their irresponsible borrowing of large sums of money they could never hope to pay back, and the power that they now had to sell off people's lifework without our being able to do *anything* came under the hammer of my anger.

The final insult came as they calmly disposed of a hundred years of Peter's family history in one go – not to one of the many reputable firms who had been trying to buy this for years, but to a company who were only too well known for not being good employers of their Indian staff, amongst whom we had many friends.

Mentally I wrote articles to the *Financial Times*, planning a full-scale exposure of this and some of their other questionable activities. But it was useless destructive anger and the only thing possible was to put it all behind us, genuinely forgiving those who had harmed us in this way, thus allowing God to open a new chapter in our lives with whatever that might involve.

3

Who I Am or What I Do

The loss of any sense of self-worth that comes with redundancy is very strong indeed, and it was only as we joined ranks with the unemployed that the full extent of the problem became apparent.

'From the moment you lose your job,' said one unemployed factory worker, 'it is almost as if you cease to exist.'

'They come out of their doors backwards,' said another, 'and people you have spent a lifetime working alongside no longer speak to you.'

Even in our own well-to-do area of the country I came across some amazing revelations the minute we were also on the dole.

One woman I had known for several years admitted that her husband had been out of work for some time, but had forbidden her to tell anyone. While she had lived with the agonising worry of coping with the family tensions and finances, he had acted out the charade of actually going up to London every day at the same time as before – rather than admit to the dreadful stigma of being out of work.

This was no isolated incident. I came across similar situations time and again.

One man we knew had lost his job because a company he had only just joined had gone into liquidation – a situation for which he could in no way be held responsible. Yet the sense of rejection almost broke him.

For a long time he would cross the road rather than speak to anyone in what he felt to be this 'naked' jobless state. Finally he deliberately left the country and started again somewhere right away from all his old friends.

Often whole families seem to go to ground during redundancy, feeling like lepers in society and no longer being able to hold their heads up with any sense of self-worth.

Even our children at school, who talked openly and without embarrassment of Dad's present lack of a job, were surprised to find that other children would admit to a similar problem in their own family – which they had previously felt too ashamed to mention.

The Status of a Job Label

For years whenever anyone asked me about myself I would respond automatically by telling them what work we did. Somewhere along the line 'who I am' has become 'what I do'. How much more devastating then to lose the only means of status I possess. By definition, being unemployed will mean that I now feel that I am 'nothing' and of no intrinsic value.

In the *British Journal of Social Psychology* it was recorded by Dr Breakwell that most unemployed people thought that others saw them

> in a much less favourable light than the employed... They really believed that others despised and deprecated them. This in itself was enough to generate discomfort, but when reinforced by other trauma associated with unemployment it can threaten the whole fabric of identity.

'Why did it happen to me?' was a refrain I heard over

and over again. However reasonable the cause of a person's loss of work, it seems he or she will inevitably feel that this must somehow be *my* failure, or *my* lack of the necessary calibre.

The Success Syndrome

Basically most people seem to feel that life is more about 'getting on' and 'succeeding' than about the essential qualities of character and personality that our faith and our humanity require of us. Even Christians admitted that status and the amount of money they earned had unconsciously assumed a higher priority in their lives than the kind of people they were at home behind closed doors.

'Money is a way of measuring how much you are worth,' said Brian. 'And the job you do tells others what your status is reckoned to be.'

Having fallen so suddenly from a life of recognisable success, John found the sense of humiliation and loss of this 'status' almost unendurable.

> You go to the Employment Exchange and you register. You become a number and just a face along with all the other faces. Faces that unlike any other gathering avoid each other because they feel ashamed. There are no smiles, no laughter, only pain and frustration. They get out of the place as soon as they can.
>
> You go to the head hunters and have to go through the indignity of having to explain what happened without being able to. The feeling is that you have become 'unclean' and somewhat of an embarrassment. It is humiliating, depressing and destructive.

It Should be Different for the Christian

A recently converted man in our congregation has written this:

> For any conscientious hard-working person the 'job' is a means of establishing an identity in society. 'I am an engineer, a postman or a chartered accountant.' These are labels or props which help the otherwise direction-less to stand on their own feet. When the job is removed the individual is found flat on his or her back, having to start afresh to build an identity. For Christians these labels are, of course, irrelevant...

Probably in essence he is right, but I have yet to find anyone for whom this is totally true. We have all swallowed the value systems of society around us and the sense of rejection in unemployment inevitably remains very strong. To the same extent that we feel insecure or unloved as people, both by God and our fellow men, we feel an equivalent loss of status on redundancy. Clearly this will be stronger for some than for others.

Chris himself actually became a Christian through the whole experience of being made redundant, and was, therefore, much more aware of the difference that his newly found faith made to the whole situation.

> How has this changed me as an individual? Enormously! Much more than may outwardly be apparent. To begin with I started to sleep well again. I stopped worrying about unemployment and debt and began to have faith that the situation would resolve itself in the way that the Lord decided and, therefore, inevitably for the better in the long run. I relaxed and regained my sense of humour. I was more tolerant and stopped judging people. I enjoyed my contacts with others

much more, and started to look outwards again rather than continually being preoccupied with my own problems.

The difference was so marked that they all thought that I must have clinched some deal – I looked so pleased with life!

For those who had already been Christians in the longer term the difference was more difficult to measure, but all of us found that our faith was a life-line in the situation – certainly we could never have coped without it.

If a Man Will Not (Cannot?) Work Let Him Not Eat

One problem for Christians is that even within our churches the Protestant work ethic still has an amazingly powerful grip. Despite all our well-meant concern about the problem, owning up to not having a job seems tantamount to admitting, 'I am living on state charity, unable to lift my head with any kind of self respect.' And this idea persists in certain areas despite unemployment figures of well over three million that should disprove it to any thinking person.

'Of course there are plenty of jobs,' said a rather pompous church lady. 'The newspapers are full of them. If people were really prepared to *look* I'm sure they could find something.'

One lovely Christian lady told me, with what I am sure was well-meant piety, how her husband had prayed about the situation and got a job the very week that his redundancy notice had come through. The implication from her critical expression was perfectly clear – 'If only *you* had more faith, like we have.'

So often the very people stuck in the dole queues are those least able to move out and look for a job. I shall never forget the few days I spent in one of the worst unemployment areas north of Birmingham, where only *one* teenager out of a whole class of school-leavers was lucky to get a proper job, and where the hopelessness in the air is really terrifying.

Somehow people all around us are having actually to cope, living with this situation every day, facing an empty future, selling up and moving to some remote location, or simply getting by under the stresses and strains of life multiplied a hundred times over - no holidays, nothing for the little extras of life, and constantly getting under each other's feet in homes that may contain unemployed school-leavers as well. Even their friends who stick by them will very likely have no idea of what they are going through.

How desperately cruel then even to *think* that these people do not really 'want' to find a job and are really scrounging on state charity!

What Value Does God Give Us?

Surely we must get back behind the automatic labelling and status seeking that goes on to the essential beliefs of our faith - that a human being is of value because of 'who' he is and not simply 'what' he does. Each one of us is an individual creation of the living God - a life of inestimable value that Jesus Himself was willing to give His own life to rescue.

One of the great distinguishing marks of the Christian faith has always been the immense value it attaches to every living person, whereas Hinduism, for example, looks only towards the goal of nirvana, where the individual will eventually be merged into eternal oblivion, and human life is seen as just one more passing reincarnation and very cheap.

Jesus Himself was always at great pains to tell His followers how much He cares for us in the here and now. 'Not one of them [a sparrow] will fall to the ground without your Father's will... you are of more value than many sparrows' (Matt. 10:29,31), and 'My sheep hear my voice, and I know them... I give them eternal life... and no one shall snatch them out of my hand' (John 10:27,28).

Is it really possible to believe that we do not matter to a God like this, and that He does not really care about our situation? Perhaps like Chris we all need to look again at the many wonderful promises in the Bible, and to learn to trust Him afresh with all our current heartache and uncertainty. He *will* see us through the difficult days ahead, making a way that we may be able to bear them, and we *can* genuinely trust Him with the fact that however black things seem at present 'in everything God works for good with those who love Him, who are called according to His purpose' (Rom. 8:28).

For our part we could never have got by without a caring church and friends who stood by us without continually asking us whether there was any sign of a job yet. Some dropped advertisements through the door with jobs that sounded possible, others introduced us to friends who could help, but most of all they were there with a loving but unobtrusive concern about how we were coping.

4

Things Ain't What They Used to Be

The root cause of the unemployed person's problem in society today is that few people actually *in* full employment have any idea of how bad the situation has become. They see the world-wide statistics in their newspapers, and continual company closures reported on television, but somehow the full implications of the situation do not impinge on their conscious minds.

When most people now over 30 left school there *were* plenty of jobs available, and one could actually choose between a variety of reasonable alternatives. Anyone unemployed in *that* situation probably could be accused of not trying hard enough, or not really wanting a job. Today the situation is light-years away from those comfortable rose-coloured days – but most people simply do not realise this.

Parents of teenage school-leavers, who themselves managed to find work with the greatest of ease, will criticise their children for 'not really wanting to find work', or 'scrounging idly on the dole'.

Young people themselves, who have been told that if they work hard enough at their exams they will get their just rewards in terms of a reasonable job, are shattered to find themselves perched precariously on some 'Youth Opportunity' scheme, with nothing else visible on the horizon. And their cry is, not unnaturally, 'Why did no one tell us how difficult it was going to be?' or 'What have we worked all these years at school to achieve?'

It is much the same for older folk who suddenly find themselves redundant. Most of their friends and colleagues still in full-time employment will not really have much idea of how difficult it has now become to get *any* job. To begin with they may be sympathetic and try to be helpful and supportive, but before long as the hundreds of job applications come to nothing, they may well begin to feel that their friend is 'not trying hard enough', or that 'surely he could get a job with his experience and qualifications.' In the end they may conclude that he must have some hidden failing that they had never recognised before – after all, in *their* experience a little bit of real effort has always produced results. Lack of understanding of the sheer magnitude of the problem usually causes sympathy to disappear rather quickly after several months in this situation.

For the unemployed person himself the situation is totally devastating. He may start out on his job search with a reasonable degree of hope and confidence (based on his earlier experience in younger days), but before long, as the applications are returned with several hundred more 'no thank yous', or, worst still, simply 'unanswered' he is increasingly filled with despair. I met several people with whole files of job rejection slips who had not surprisingly just given up.

Techniques Must Change with the Times

In every age the situation has changed so drastically that a totally new approach has become essential – one that simply *has* to be taken on board by young and old alike.

Stephen returned from several years of successful accountancy work in Africa, conscious of the needs of his young children to go to school in their own home country.

With his good qualifications and plenty of experience behind him, he made the fatal mistake of assuming that this would land him a reasonable job in the UK in only a few weeks or months. Moreover, since he was also a committed Christian, he automatically assumed that the Lord would provide. It was only after many months of applying for job after job and just occasionally ending up on the final short list, but all to no avail, that he began to realise that he was getting nowhere fast.

Mike had just graduated with a really good degree, which until a few years ago would have got him an excellent job with a variety of different organisations. But as he wrote round to all these firms, after leaving university, he was shattered at the number of polite refusals he received. Five hundred graduates were often chasing just three or four jobs, and he subsequently discovered that those who had been successful had started their job search very early in the *previous* year, leaving no stone unturned.

Jane is in an even worse situation. She has a few CSEs and O-levels, but as she applies for job after job, she quickly realises that her potential employers have the pick of the town at their disposal. Supermarket tills are frequently manned by graduates and high-fliers, who would previously never have looked at these jobs. She is rapidly realising that to have left her education where she did, and not to have worked towards a definite goal, was little short of lethal in today's job market.

A New Approach

However difficult it seems for all of us, we are going to have to start much earlier to assess our gifts and abilities with confidence, and to work much harder at learning to set out positively on the job search.

After many months of doggedly applying for job after job in the accountancy world, it was finally borne in on Stephen that somewhere he had got it wrong. The old-style formal application stating in a fairly low key and British way the bald facts of his experience and qualifications was clearly not even getting a look in.

Although in every way it went against the grain, he was going to have to learn to 'sell' himself and his abilities positively and completely reword his c.v. before *anything* was likely to happen. Moreover his faith and trust in God was not going to act as some kind of invisible insurance policy. Other people around him were going through exactly the same problems, and Christians had not been promised any kind of exemption certificate. It was not blind faith but sensible action which God could support that was required.

After only a few weeks with a local career counsellor, who also turned out to be a Christian, he began completely to reassess his abilities and his strong points, and to gain the confidence to set himself up in a consultancy partnership which is now steadily growing from strength to strength. It was thanks to our encountering Stephen fairly early in Peter's job search that we were set on the right rails in looking for professional help, which we might otherwise have regarded as completely unnecessary.

Retraining and Professional Help

Many companies making employees redundant can be made to pay for these people to go to a professional career consultant or for some kind of retraining. Some of the better companies do this voluntarily and automatically.

There is a wide variety of different consultancy firms operating in this field, and it pays to do plenty of research into what they offer beforehand, since, if you should have the misfortune to have to pay for this yourself, they are far from cheap.

Their primary function is to take you in hand and to assess your work and ability potential – which will almost certainly be much wider and more saleable than you had previously thought. They undertake to stay with you and help and encourage you throughout your time of unemployment, suggesting a variety of avenues for you to try, pointing out appropriate advertisements and even sending you for interviews with people they think can help.

During all this time they will drill into you some positive thinking about the abilities and experience you have, which will be very necessary if, as is often the case, your confidence has received a fair bashing because of being made redundant in the first place. You will, or you should, get some intensive training in interview techniques, which will probably include tape or video recordings, so that you can see for yourself how you come over to a potential employer. They will also reword your c.v. for you, and help you to apply positively and enthusiastically for the appropriate jobs that are advertised as well as writing 'blind' to firms that might possibly be interested in your skills.

However, in case you are despairing that you cannot possibly afford the services of such a firm, let me say two things at this point.

First, in the United Kingdom at least, there is a very efficient network of government-provided groups operating throughout the country, which offer similar services virtually free – although, of course, for a wider group of people and less individually orientated. Several of these groups are very good indeed and have the added advantage that members are able to help and encourage one another. Again it pays to ask around about which are the better centres, since one or two people have found it more beneficial to travel to a neighbouring area.

Second, you might possibly be the kind of person who does not actually need much of this kind of help, but who can do quite a lot of spadework for yourself using the many publications that are now available, although I personally think it pays not to be over-confident about this unless you are exceptionally strong and well motivated. One of the very real dangers as time goes by and the rejection slips come rolling in, is that apathy and depression can set in.

Getting Going

It takes a while to get into gear over your job search. I remember listening with incredulity to Stephen when he first told us about all the work involved. 'Get out the typewriter, get working on your c.v., and get stripped ready for action,' was his advice. 'What on earth is he talking about?' I thought. But we soon found out!

First, you will need to write out a positive and fully informative c.v. listing not only qualifications but also any relevant job experience you may have that pertains to the post being advertised.

It is *not* enough to write one blanket c.v. for all purposes, and you will often need to rewrite this, with particular emphasis on any and every aspect of the experience you have that is relevant for the job being advertised. Sometimes this may mean rewriting your c.v. individually for each post, but for others one c.v. will do for one category of work opportunities.

Since employers will often be receiving many hundreds of these applications when advertising any job, it is essential to keep the length of your c.v. down to a reasonable minimum while still telling them all they need to know about you. In other words it is necessary to use a few well-chosen impact making sentences that contain a lot of information, thus keeping the reader's attention and arousing his interest. If you are no good with words then this is something you will definitely need help over.

In addition to jobs actually being advertised there is another whole area of work possibility available. Once you have worked out your basic skills and job experience (more about this in the chapter on new beginnings), then the next step will be to look up the names of firms anywhere in the area who may conceivably have a use for the work experience you have to offer and write to them about your interest and availability. You can find these firms listed in the files of your local library, and although it involves a lot of painstaking research the effort is very definitely worth-while. Peter had a number of interested replies from such approaches.

Finding the Help You Need

When looking for personal help among your friends and neighbours, it is good to choose just a few people whom you really like and trust. However bad you may be feeling at times, it does not pay to go on about this to everyone you meet. People find it embarrassing, and, just as in a bereavment situation they will probably not know what to say or how to help. (More about this in Chapter 2). In the end you may find them avoiding you!

John's advice in the situation was to tell a few well-chosen friends, asking them to pray for you and keeping them informed of the circumstances – but then to say no more about the subject except when asked.

If you look around among your friends, you will probably be able to think of certain people who could help by introducing you to others in a relevant line of employment, or could even themselves be of help. Again make this a fairly low-key approach, underlining the fact that you do not expect *them* to offer you a job, but only to seek their advice. Most people are only too happy to do what they can to help and Peter was given a number of really useful contacts in this way. The best approach is by letter, saying that you will get in touch with them at a later date to see if they have any useful ideas or feel they can help in any way – thus allowing them a comfortable and easy way out if they feel at all pressurised or embarrassed. In fact, everyone we approached proved more than willing to be consulted in this way.

5

Time on Your Hands

The desperate mother of an out-of-work teenager:

> I simply can't get him out of bed. He just lazes around all day getting under my feet, and not making any effort to help or find himself a job.

A machine-tool worker who had been on the dole several years previously:

> I used to sit in front of the window day after day, just gazing up at the sky and thinking, 'Tomorrow I'll do something. Tomorrow it will be different.' Before, I used to paint a lot, but now that I had the time, I couldn't bring myself to do it. I would even analyse the scene and think about how to draw it, but all the enthusiasm and energy seemed to have gone out of me. Looking back, I simply can't believe how much time I spent just sitting around, watching television and doing nothing. There seemed to be nothing to get up for, and nothing to do if I did.

Probably for all the years that we were slogging away at school, or completely taken up with a full-time job, with leisure time and holidays at an absolute premium, our one great dream may very well have been to have 'more time'. Time to do all those things we have been longing to try, to stop and think occasionally, or just to relax and enjoy life a bit more.

But once that time is actually there, endlessly, week after week and month after month, the picture becomes very different from what we had imagined.

I was fortunate in that Peter actually enjoyed being at home, and could find more than enough to do with his leisure hours. The problem was that he really needed most of that time for a fairly intensive job-search programme, and that, anyway, many of the things we had dreamt of doing with our leisure hours needed money – and the money we had would need to be saved for the rainy days ahead.

Plenty of Time, But No Money

Needless to say, this is the heart of the problem for most people – especially for youngsters who have no money saved anyway, or for those who were already living from hand to mouth and just about making ends meet before redundancy struck.

Youngsters on the dole, who get what many people regard as quite a handsome sum of 'pocket-money' each week, have a particular problem with this. Most of them contribute towards the cost of their keep at home, and then when they have paid their fares to almost anywhere, or gone out for a single evening then there is nothing left to spend on the hours of leisure that stretch before them each week.

Older folk with redundancy pay in their pockets will often be tempted to spend this on a really good holiday or something they have always wanted, and then later when the bills mount up they wish they had kept something by to make the occasional break possible. Of course, there are plenty of things you can do without money, especially in the country, but in the bleak, treeless inner-city areas where unemployment is at its highest, hanging around a concrete yard or a derelict bombsite, or just sitting at home watching the television are real recipes for despair.

The Priority of Getting Organised

As I discovered years ago, when starting to work from home as a freelance writer, having 'all day' to get things done is a fatal recipe for inactivity, unless you learn to be really tough with yourself.

Parkinson's law, where the little old lady staying down in Brighton takes all day to write three postcards *because she has all day*, quickly comes into operation. Moreover, the sense of hopelessness that unemployment frequently brings with it as an extra millstone, can quickly produce a state of apathy unless we get a grip of ourselves. Nearly all the people I talked to found it difficult to keep themselves going each day without help from outside.

A Regular Working Day

Unending time like this is something you have to get by the scruff of the neck from the outset. Most people find it works best if they set themselves regular working hours, just as if they were actually still employed. Providing that they are sufficiently tough with themselves, this will then get them out of bed instead of lounging around – and it will come to an end at the appropriate time, too, rather than dragging on into the small hours.

The tendency is either to procrastinate by finding all kinds of other things that need doing around the house, thus simply pottering around all day and achieving nothing. Or else almost to drown in the pressure of the job search.

At one point Peter got so bogged down in the pressure of it all that the whole family was living with this 'morning, noon and night' without any relief.

Use proper working hours to go through advertisements; work at rewriting your c.v.; do research into firms in the area that you could write to; and then take time to relax and put it all away for the evening. It is absolutely essential to get the right balance.

Also, if at all possible, the ideal is actually to work in a room set aside for the purpose – again, so that this can literally be left behind when working hours are over.

Unfortunately, whatever is or is not available in terms of room to work in, many men like to work in the comfort of the main living-room area so that life has to revolve around them. But, of course, this means that all the evidence of unemployment pressure is constantly around for everyone, including family and friends, to see – thus making it impossible ever to forget or relax.

Finding Other Interests

As I said earlier one of the most pressing needs of the unemployed person is to get out of the house and do something completely different, if possible on a regular basis. Anything that requires physical activity or a mental break from the situation and away from the pressures of home life will do.

Many people have taken to regular sporting activities such as jogging, which helps to combat lethargy and depression in, quite literally, working off the feelings. Others have taken up social and charitable work which is of great benefit to the area. Whole new projects have been started by out-of-work people in this way, and I have often wondered if God is not using this situation to open people's eyes to the needs of others around them.

Peter got involved in raising funds for a large new youth centre in one of the most deprived areas of London. It was a Christian project already stretched to the full through lack of space and the need was desperate. He had never done this kind of thing before and the challenge really gripped him. It was also a very salutary experience when he was feeling down to see that others were living with worse problems than he was. Only recently we heard that the centre had actually received enough money to start building work much earlier than they expected, and with more than they had dared for within this time scale.

I heard similar stories time and again, as people had gone out of their own homes looking for things to do to help *other* people in need – disabled children, old folk, charities in need of business and financial advice, Rotary projects, new church buildings. The list seemed endless.

Not Total Distraction

There is, of course, a corresponding danger, which is that this kind of work can become so rewarding in itself that it can completely distract the unemployed person from his necessary job search. Again this is a matter for balance and a regular timetable.

One man became so absorbed in his work for the local children's home that he devoted every moment of the day to this, while his job search and the funds that his family so badly needed were completely forgotten.

Clearly there will be times when God has specifically called us to this kind of work and then we can trust Him for all our needs, but unless this is the case, then such full-time preoccupation can be a fatal avoidance of the task in hand.

At the other extreme Jim was so worried about the family financial situation that he refused to get involved with *any* work outside his job search – unless it was paid for. This was, needless to say, totally self-defeating, because he got himself and the family totally bogged down in his own problems. As Christians we have been commanded not to be 'anxious', but just to keep on trusting – and to keep on looking.

6

The Support Group

Applying for jobs and trying 'to sell' yourself can be a very traumatic business if you have never really had to do this before. After the first few refusal slips, or worse still unanswered letters, you can very quickly find yourself in the pits of despair.

Chris describes himself as a fairly resilient type of person. He did his own research, designed and improved his own c.v., refined a special 'pushy' letter and got moving. Out went the letters and in came the interview invitations. 'It's only a matter of time,' he thought.

> Three hundred letters and sixty interviews later and still no viable job. I was thinking I should change my deodorant yet again, rethink my taste in ties, and invest in some plastic surgery and a prolonged course with the psychologist! Six weeks from unemployment and I was resigned to a long spell of unpaid leisure and was reassessing the family's future life style. The house was up for sale for a more modest habitation. I kept waking up in the middle of the night, sweating at the thought of all those bills to pay and no monthly pay cheque. My wife was as close to a mental breakdown as I ever wish to see again, and the whole family was suffering from the tensions.

Robert told me:

I would just sit looking at this great pile of advertisements in the paper and wonder if I could face writing yet another batch of fruitless letters. It is no longer possible to convince yourself that it is worth going on and on. Somewhere between the telephone and the typewriter hope dies.

At this point just about everyone needs the help and support of a group of people in the same situation, who can identify with each other's problems without feeling embarrassed, and above all keep each other up to the mark.

Andrew has been out of work for nearly two years, and he freely admits that if he had persisted with the PER group in his area, or if there had been some kind of group for unemployed people at the church he attends, then he would have got on with his job search with much greater determination. He knows he needs others to keep him up to the mark, but at the same time he has discovered how much easier it is to distract himself and to find other things to do with his time.

Men in particular find it very difficult to talk about what is going on for them, and it is only within ther safety of a group where everyone, except possibly the leader, is in the same boat that they are remotely likely to risk showing their vulnerability in this way. Even then they may need a fair amount of persuasion even to consider the prospect!

Peter had certainly been helped by the career consultant whose services had been paid for as a part of his redundancy package. But eventually I think it was the experience of the local executive sharing group that finally set him free from the prison of his own fears and needs.

The realisation that there in prosperous suburban Surrey there were *others* going through exactly the same desperate struggles, with identical feelings of failure and inadequacy, finally proved to him that he was not alone. Other people needed *his* help and support as much as he needed theirs.

A Group for Every Situation

Such groups come in all shapes and sizes, from unemployment black spots like Liverpool and Walsall to the so-called stockbroker belt around Horsham and Guildford, and in my opinion they are a major way in which churches which do not already operate such groups can be of real practical help. They may be run by management consultants, social workers, or trained church folk, but always this kind of peer group support is proving the most liberating and fulfilling help to the unemployed, even in the really depressed areas where this will probably never lead to another job.

A young professional man wrote to the management consultant running his executive sharing group in these terms:

> Although the job I finally found had very little to do with the work that we actually did in the group, I look back on the days that we met with nothing but gratitude. It was well worth the experience of redundancy, traumas and all, just to have discovered what it means really to be helped and supported by others in the same situation – men who I would never have dreamt could care about me to this extent.

When I suggested a group like this to a gathering of machine-tool workers who had been out of work for many months previously, they were scornful and virtually laughed in my face. 'What good would tea and sympathy have done?' was their very natural reaction. But as we sat and talked, officially doing research for my book, I was able to get them to talk more freely about their experiences, their resentments against unions and management, and their hopes and fears for the future.

When they had been hard at it for over an hour, I asked them the same question,

'If you had had this kind of a group when you were actually out of work, would you have found it a help?'

'Well, if you mean *this* kind of a group – yes, certainly.'
'I've never talked like this to anyone before.'
'I never knew my friend had the same kind of problems.'
'I always felt so alone.'

And so it went on.

Not far down the road, under the auspices of a lovely rotund church-worker, a similar group had actually been operating for nearly eighteen months. All of them had gone to the group in a final last-ditch effort to find a job and full of apprehension about whether it was some kind of 'church plot'. None of them had ever spoken to each other before in their lives.

Now every single one of them looked on the experience as a major turning-point. They met two or three times a week, doing everything from learning to paint to laying stone walls. Above all they had become really firm friends, helping and supporting one another in all the inevitable problems of living with unemployment.

Because most of these men were over 50, as well as living in a really depressed area, they had no real chance of ever finding a job – but it didn't seem to matter so much any more. They had found each other, and some of them had found faith. Above all they had begun to feel of some value in the world.

Keeping Each Other Going

While it is relatively easy to kid yourself and other people around you that you are really working at the job-search programme ('Recently I've just been a little bit tired or under the weather, that's all. I'll get on with it next week...'), other people in the same boat are not so easily fooled. Rather like members in a group such as Alcoholics Anonymous, they are only too well aware of the little excuses we manage to make to ourselves at such times!

Keeping people up to the mark in the job search when they are quietly sinking down into apathy and despair is one of the main functions of this kind of group. By definition there is always someone in a 'better place' present who can see what is really going on.

Then again there is the obvious fact that several heads are better than one when it comes to analysing talents and motivation. As they talked around the group about past training and experience there was nearly always someone to ask, 'Well, why haven't you thought of looking in that direction then?' indicating a whole area of experience that the speaker had quickly glossed over and almost forgotten.

One man I met had completely changed the direction of his career through such a challenge. While he was speaking about his engineering work in the oil industry there was a lack-lustre air about his whole demeanour. Then he touched briefly on another hobby that obviously totally fascinated him so that his whole being lit up with animation.

One of his colleagues in the group asked,

> Has it ever occurred to you that there could well be a ready market for your knowledge and expertise in the adult education sector? Perhaps it wouldn't bring in a full living wage, but it's blindingly obvious to me that you would really enjoy this – and you could always use your engineering experience in a consultancy capacity to make up your income.

George has never looked back since the day that

suggestion was made and he admits that he would never have thought of it himself in a thousand years! Today he counts his redundancy a real blessing in disguise. Although he is not earning as much as before, he has *never* enjoyed his everyday work so much.

One management consultant running such a group said that he never failed to be fascinated by things that were said during the times that they met. 'You wouldn't believe the way they speak to one another,' he said. 'They often come out with things that I would never dare to say. But being in the same situation they really know each other's problems – and they are nearly always right!'

A Reason to Get Out of the House

Quite apart from these obvious benefits of help and friendship, a regular meeting for the unemployed person gives him a reason and a purpose for getting out of the house – and therefore away from the temptation of sitting brooding over the problem all by himself.

This is even more necessary if the home is very small and already housing out-of-work teenage children or noisy little ones! Career consultants and social workers all agreed that one of the primary benefits of the time that unemployed people spent with them was that it got them out of what had often become a very tense home situation.

Everyone I talked to who was in any way involved with these groups or drop-in centres said what an absolute lifeline they had been – something to look forward to, a chance to meet other people, a breath of fresh air, and a ray of hope to hold on to.

The Christian Support Group

As you would expect, the Christian support group which

also meets to pray has proved one of the most effective in the life of the unemployed.

During the course of my research I came across Stephen, a professional career consultant, who had felt it right to offer much of his leisure time to helping unemployed people in the London area around his home church. All the techniques and skills which he used every day for his work were thus available to those who probably could never have afforded them professionally.

In addition, this group was to be run as a Christian fellowship in its own right, where people could share their needs and problems but also pray for each other.

When I bumped into him several months later, I asked him how it was going – 'Oh it's finished' he said. Then seeing the puzzled look on my face, 'What I mean is that all the members of that particular group have now found work: *we're* actually starting again in a few weeks' time.'

Again in the UK, Church Action with the Unemployed have set up centres and contact persons across the country. Obviously a great deal more is still needed, but these projects are growing rapidly, and in most parts of the country the Church has become very heavily employed in helping unemployed people.

Wanting to Forget

One very real problem for groups helping with unemployed people is that from the moment their members find work they simply do not want to be involved any more. It is a very natural reaction. The pain and rejection involved in the downtime of unemployment, most vividly portrayed in the BBC series 'Boys from the Blackstuff', is so bitter that once this period is behind you, with all your heart you want to forget all about it.

As a result people who have been an integral part of the

group and a great help and support to the others will suddenly disappear, thus adding to the rejection of those left behind. In addition, all that they have learnt is lost to the group.

In fact it is a common assumption that once you are back in full-time employment the whole gruesome subject of downtime can be put out of sight. Even Hodder's asked me whether I still wanted to write this book, once we were through the wood!

I did not *want* to write it, but then I remembered that we are called 'to help others also' with the help that we have been given.

7

New Beginnings

When you have been doing the same kind of work for years as Peter had, it can be very difficult to carry out any kind of constructive 'rethink'. His accountancy training, used largely as a background for general business practice, was getting a little rusty – not unlike schoolboy French, as his career counsellor tactfully put it! And for twenty years he had been involved in the management and administration of tropical-type agricultural projects.

On paper this inevitably came out as 'overseas only' experience, despite the fact that for six to nine months of the year the work had been done from London. But very early on in his job search Peter had made up his mind that he did not want to work overseas again, so that door seemed to be shut. But where did we go from there?

However devastating the initial impact of redundancy, it is vital to take the opportunity that the situation offers, rather than grasping at the first panic solution that comes along. Very possibly this will be the *one opportunity* in your life to stop and take stock of where you are going and why – a breathing-space from the rat race and, above all, a chance to hear what God is saying to you personally. We came across plenty of people who had never looked back from what had seemed a real tragedy at the time. Paul Tournier's book, *Adventure in Living*, can be a very positive source of inspiration along these lines.

Discovering Your Basic Success Drives

One of the most helpful exercises in finding the way ahead and the right direction for any new beginning is a technique frequently used by groups and career consultants. You can find the nuts and bolts of this laid out in Bernard Haldane's book, *How to make a Habit of Success* (Warner Books).

List in some detail the twenty achievements in your life from which you found the greatest fulfilment. These do *not* have to be anything major, and can include quite simple things from making something practical with your hands in the home to winning some small prize at school, organising a new local chamber of commerce to streamlining a company's profitability potential. Anything goes in the exercise, and often it is the smaller, less obvious successes of life which can give the biggest clues about where our gifts really lie. The most important thing is to be completely honest about the things that *you* (and not other people) have found really satisfying and fulfilling.

When you have finished, cut this list down to roughly ten achievements that you personally would put top of the list, and then grade these down in order of preference numerically. Write down every little detail about each of these ten successes, looking to see what skills and abilities were involved. Finally, take note of the skills that all these achievements have *in common*, and a very interesting pattern will begin to emerge.

In Peter's case things like management, administration, finance and negotiating came out on top every time, going right back to his early school-life, his time in the army during national service, and even in the local church.

For me every single achievement which gave me real satisfaction came at a point where words and communication generally overlapped with helping and relating to people – which at least showed me that I had been on roughly the right track for some time!

When you have identified the common denominators within these ten successes that you personally rate the most satisfying, you are getting close to the heart of the matter – in other words to discovering your basic motivating drives and genuine God-given talents, or what Haldane would call your 'Dynamic Success Drives'.

Out of the Strait-jacket

The problem for many people – men especially – is that they can get trapped fairly early into strait-jacket careers that are not necessarily what they are most gifted for, and which they may not even find very fulfilling. From time to time I had come across people who so hated their everyday work that they could not wait to retire, and it had always struck me what a sad waste of time and talent that was.

However unwelcome redundancy may be, it is at least a chance to stop and take a closer look at where you are trying to go and why. Sometimes an analysis of the past few years can show up quite a frightening deviation from your genuine motivating drives, and this may well indicate something you should try to avoid in future if at all possible.

The other side of the same coin, which is especially relevant in a time of high unemployment, is the need to be *flexible* and open to *many different* areas of work, which may still have the same common denominators, though appearing to be very different at first glance.

I have always tried to encourage our children to take an interest in and develop as many skills as they possibly can. In the world of the future we may have to change jobs many times and to make use of all the talents we possess instead of just a few.

Someone who is capable of management and administration with a financial bias should be able to put their skills into operation for almost any kind of organisation. Someone with caring and helping skills can also go up a great variety of avenues. The secret is to see where your gifts and your genuine motivating drives lie thickest on the ground.

The snag for the older person out of work is that although he or she may be prepared to move into a completely different industry or area where basic skills seem to fit, potential employers will probably not see it that way.

As a general rule the longer you have been up one particular tree the more you are stuck with whatever fruit it grows! And after the age of 45 employers will not generally consider *any* change of direction however superficial.

None the less I really believe that assessing your basic gifts and motivations is vital, if only to prevent your charging off on some panic solution to the problem.

Instant 'Solutions'

Wherever you go in the underworld of the unemployed you come across panic solutions that all too frequently end in disaster. One of the commonest of these is the bright, new small-business project, set up with what little redundancy pay a man has in his pocket for the future and often lost quickly. Over 40 per cent of new businesses go to the wall in this way – usually for want of proper information and market research.

Christians are by no means exempt from the problem. I met one man who had kept on doggedly losing everything on one bright idea after another, convinced that he had the necessary guidance, while his wife was out flogging herself into the ground with catering and cleaning jobs in an effort to keep the home going.

With his flair for management and administration, the idea of a small business greatly appealed to Peter, but the trouble was that he had no clear idea of what this should be.

For a number of years I had been importing and selling Indian handicrafts for an out-of-work couple in New Delhi. It was something I had really wanted to do, but I had taken it on when my time was already over-full because I could not refuse them in their time of need. Generally speaking it had been a millstone round my neck (it was certainly not on my basic talent curve!) and we had never made a profitable business out of it, though, to be fair, we had not really been trying very hard, since the whole project was set up primarily to help friends in trouble.

Was there a possibility of enlarging this into a full-scale business? I have to confess that my heart sank at the prospect. We had no retail outlet and effectively it would have meant flogging the goods around all the church and charity sales in the area, often with very little hope of success, or persuading friends to have sales in their homes on our behalf, which always made me feel guilty, although it was for a very good cause.

Many unemployed people get trapped into this sort of situation. One woman we met was attempting to sell vitamin tablets and health foods to all her friends, until both she and they began to get decidedly edgy about the situation. Another man we know had gone into the difficult and competitive life-insurance business, and since this starts best by working your way around your friends and neighbours to get them to take out policies, he was rapidly running out of friends as well!

All such projects really have to be examined very thoroughly before making a start. They may sound like good ideas at the time, but apart from giving us something to do with the many hours of empty leisure that stretch before us, they can also have frustrating and difficult side-effects.

As far as we were concerned, selling imported Indian handicrafts was not a great success, and although we increased the business tenfold, we had still scarcely struggled into the black. This did not seem to be God's way forward.

A Different Direction Altogether?

At this point in his life, and with a reasonable redundancy settlement under his belt, Peter was encouraged by one of our Christian friends who was a management consultant to take a fresh look at the possibilities.

Did he really need to work full time, or could he get by on a part-time basis? Unfortunately, with our children still not through school, the mortgage uncompleted, and pension prospects now decidedly thin, we were not really in a position to consider that. Just a few more years and we should have jumped at the chance.

One or two people we knew had been offered early retirement on a full pension and, knowing that their future was provided for, had gone wholeheartedly into helping out with one or other Christian projects. God was clearly using the situation as a way to move the gifts and talents out into the areas where they were most needed.

An accountant we know is now running the financial affairs of Operation Mobilisation; a friend from the Foreign Office who had had to leave a high-pressure job because of ill health turned his gifts and energies over to the service of World Vision; a redundant sales manager who had lost his job several years previously put the time to good use getting a Christian newspaper back on to a sound financial basis. And so it went on.

Was this the way ahead for Peter? Because of the commitments we still had to meet we were unsure. And as usual the only way was to push the door and see if it opened. It did begin to open more than a crack, but then was shut again fairly dramatically, making the situation quite clear to us. The job hunt had to go on.

8

For-the Wife

Devastating as unemployment undoubtedly is for the man of the house, I often wondered if it was not even worse for his wife and the mother of his children.

As marriages crack and break under the strain, and teenagers fight with their uncomprehending parents, the four walls of our little boxes often give no clue as to what is going on inside until it is almost too late.

When the work which normally fills our day nicely with activity, interest and comradeship is suddenly no longer available, the void returns home to roost, with all its hurts and pressures. Teenagers lie around until midday because there is no point in getting out of bed; father fills the house with his papers and endless job applications, or sits watching the television in what is often the only habitable room, and mother no longer has a moment's peace or break from it all to find the strength to cope.

The problem is that loyalty often prevents people from seeking the help and support they so much need. Wives protect husbands, and parents protect children until the strain becomes almost unbearable.

I remember just longing for someone to ask *me* how *I* was coping with it all, rather than only enquiring yet again how Peter was. Of course I was desperately concerned about him and what he was going through, but I had to live with the burden of this all day every day, and quite honestly there were days when I nearly drowned without trace.

While I had to stand by and watch helplessly his dismay at the job rejection slips, there was really very little I could *do* to ease the pain for him. At the same time I knew he needed my help and encouragement to keep going. Much of the time I felt the hopelessness of it all so strongly that I even wondered how I should be able to keep going.

As another friend in the same situation said, 'The man has at least got something to get on with, working out his notice, or going to look for work. For a wife at home, perhaps with nothing but a bucket of nappies to occupy her mind, the worries become larger than Mount Everest.'

One woman I met told me how she used to steam the letters open and then hide them away until such time as she felt that she was strong enough to help her husband cope with the rejection problem.

As far as possible I found myself falling over backwards to protect the whole family from the fall-out effect of the situation. 'Keep cheerful, put a brave face on it. Have faith that God will see us through.' But deep down inside I was screaming, 'Get me out of here, I can't cope another day without help.'

Countless women I talked to admitted rather shamefacedly to the same problems.

Sylvia had finally begged Stephen to understand that she needed a couple of mornings off a week just to get out and do something different with a girlfriend – time to offload some of her own needs and worries and just to get a break, away from the whole situation.

Jane had taken on a full-time job – just *any* job – to get her out of the house and away from it all.

Sarah was trapped with small children on her hands all day, but the marriage was deteriorating rapidly as John offloaded his anger and frustration about the situation within the safety of his own home.

As so often happens, Christians seem to suffer as much if not more than their non-Christian friends, mainly because of their tremendous guilt feelings about admitting to any real anxiety about the problem. But more than anything at this time we need the encouragement and support of loving Christian friends who will listen *without criticism or judgment* to our negative feelings and hurts: we cannot cope alone and we are not meant to. It is really a question of suffering with those who suffer, as we have been commanded to do.

During this time in our lives we quickly discovered which of our Christian friends had taken the 'love' commandments of God on board and were living them out in real terms – those who were always there when we needed them, feeling the hurts with us and obviously caring deeply about all that was happening.

Talking It Out

Alas, true Anglo-Saxon reserve so often gets in the way and prevents our talking about how bad things *really* are, either to our friends or to our husbands – and this, with a very natural family loyalty, can stop us from seeking the help we most need.

Looking back now I am appalled that I, as a trained counsellor, ever allowed myself to get into that state – I who had always advocated talking through every difficult situation and meeting one another's needs.

Why did I suddenly shoulder the burden again single handed? Certainly I could and did talk to God about it, which proved to be the greatest ongoing strength of all. But so far as most of my Christian friends were concerned I shared very little at the time, probably because instinctively I knew that most of them would not really understand.

In retrospect I am aware that I also shared far too little of my deeper feelings about the situation with Peter. I honestly believe it would have been much more help to him if I had, thus allowing him to help me as well. The more I tried to be strong and to help him, overlooking my own needs until it was almost too late, the more I encouraged him to become preoccupied with his own and, of course, the more I resented this. Judging by the many people I have talked to this is a very common problem for women during redundancy.

In actual fact, making a very needy cry for help can be just what some husbands need at such a time to restore their own self-respect and strength – if nothing else it can pull them out of their own troubles for a while.

Bringing God's Help to Others

Both the husband and the wife need loving supportive *outside* help at this time in their lives and we need to be aware of this with friends both inside and outside the church family. Listen to the testimony of Anne, a woman living close to us who was not a Christian and whom I did not know at the time:

> I suffered terribly from inadequacy and an inability to do *anything*. For a while I went through a stage when I was sure we could cope somehow. But then I had more rational moments (which became less and less frequent) as I realised that we could not possibly keep five children on nothing but food from our garden, and even an adult bicycle would not transport us all...!
>
> After the disbelief and the anger came the depression. Although I knew Chris was working very hard applying for jobs, I took each rejection letter as another personal rebuke. I was getting very weepy about the place.
>
> Basically nobody helped. The odd person said

cheerfully 'Oh something will come up' - *and that certainly didn't help.* Most friends were rather embarrassed and almost tried to avoid us. I can certainly say that you know who your friends are in a time of crisis - and it's surprising who does turn up trumps.

I can't in all honesty say that it was my Christian friends who were a help at the time, and of course at that time I was still not a Christian myself. I certainly feel that there were those who could have told me about the love and strength of God in that situation. I know the problem of talking to non-Christian friends about this, but all the same I hope and pray that when I meet people in times of need like this, I shall be able to witness to them about how much God has helped me.

In fact it was Chris, my non-Christian husband, who in sheer desperation at my depression said to me one day, 'Oh for goodness' sake, I'm doing all I can. Pull yourself together, go to the doctor and get a sedative. Or go to church and pray or *something.*' As it turned out that was the beginning of a completely new life for both of us.

9

Role Swapping, or Who Pays the Bills?

Many women I met were out at work earning while their husbands were stuck at home slumped in front of the television set, feeling utterly dejected and of no value. This was particularly true of the older men who had been brought up to believe that it was the 'role' of the husband to bring home the money and pay the bills. Nearly all of them said how humiliating they found it to be kept by their wives, and, worse still, to have to ask them for pocket-money simply because they themselves could not get a job.

Correspondingly, the women themselves were often bitter and resentful at having to be out earning while their husbands were apparently doing nothing at home. Often they felt landed with both the job and the housework, and the tensions building up inside the home were on a knife-edge.

There is a lot of glib simplistic talk about this kind of role-swapping, particularly among Chritians, and we need to beware. Remarks like, 'If only all the women would give up their jobs then there would be enough for the men,' can be like a red rag to an angry bull.

In all probability the man has already been out tramping round the job centres and knocking on doors for weeks. The fact that there are women in these jobs usually means that the jobs are specially suited to them and men would not be taken on even if they applied.

In the UK it often means that things are taken care of by

social security. If the wife is earning, she is not allowed to receive more than a small amount, which is deducted from unemployment benefit. Statistics record that many women in this predicament have been forced to give up work shortly after their husbands were made redundant, thus adding to home tensions and feelings of bitterness.

For several years I had earned a certain amount, mainly as a writer and broadcaster, but it was certainly not enough to pay the bills. Inevitably the question came up for us, too. Should I look for a full-time job, thus officially becoming the breadwinner? Peter was convinced that my talents and experience were more saleable than his, but I was very unsure about the whole issue.

Although Peter *said* he would not mind, I had serious doubts about whether in fact this would be the case when it came to the point. I knew only too well from my counselling work that it takes a very secure man indeed, sure in his own identity, not to feel very inadequate, and I had met several couples for whom this had spelt disaster – even though it had seemed the only answer at the time.

When I eventually agreed to apply, the only two jobs that came close to actuality were such that would have soaked up every second of my time and energy and left me without anything to give to Peter and the family, let alone the house.

It would doubtless have been interesting to be broadcasting officer for the Church of England, but my relief when I failed the final short list gave me a fair indication of the pressure that I really felt about the job. And, indeed, the two friends that I had asked for references had tactfully tried to indicate their concern about how on earth I would cope with the enormous time pressures.

Then there was another very full-time post as personnel manager for an independent television company which promised even more pressure. Leaving home on the commuter train at 7.30 a.m. and getting back twelve hours later seemed the ultimate in total exhaustion, especially when I would almost inevitably be returning to homework, cooking and the kitchen sink. What little I had seen of role swapping seldom seemed to extend to this kind of function, let alone coping with all the usual family problems and other odd things.

But what really was right? Peter's primary concern was not unnaturally that one of us should bring home the cash to pay the bills, and not worry about all the other issues till later.

I felt totally trapped between feeling that I would have to take the job, but, equally, that I had no idea how I should cope and wondering more than anything what my taking on such a position would do to Peter's morale.

I took a quick sideways glance at Jenny, who had started a fairly hectic job locally some years previously when her husband had been put on part-time work. The hours were nothing like as bad as those which had now come on to my horizon, but even so she had been finding it a tremendous effort to return home to a pile of housework, and despite all her husband's good intentions she got precious little help with this.

After barely a year he was working only when something 'came up', and it was almost as if he had ceased to care now that she had become the main breadwinner. He would just sit around all day waiting for her to come home and cook for him and their three children. Needless to say, Jenny could not help resenting this, but nothing she said seemed to make any difference.

At the time she first took on the job he had seemed very much in favour of the whole idea but, looking back, she was aware that their relationship had changed dramatically for the worse since then.

Of course, there are couples for whom this can work and work well, but in each case the individuals involved are very secure people who are able to communicate openly and honestly about their feelings and needs. There is nearly always a certain amount of pain involved, especially for the man.

This is gradually changing, but attitudes and expectations are often so deeply rooted that the hurt and the bitterness are very strong indeed.

As I pointed out in my book *Today's Christian Woman* these attitudes are largely hangovers from Victorian days, and there is nothing necessarily Christian or 'right' about saying that women shouldn't work. In previous generations both men and women were often out earning money for the family as a matter of course.

A new generation of younger folk living with the continuing problem of unemployment will obviously have to take completely different attitudes on board and learn to share and support each other. Indeed, the signs are that this is already happening.

10

Unemployment – What Can We Do to Help?

While people are rightly lobbying the government 'to do something' about the state of unemployment, I have already seen that there is a great deal that genuinely concerned people can do to help without waiting for others to act. If we are not careful, leaving it all to those with political clout can develop into an easy way out of taking any responsibility. Just think what would have happened if Wilberforce or Shaftesbury had taken that line!

Talking to some of the young people in the hardest hit areas I quickly discovered that they had lost faith in *any* political party and in government as a whole to solve their problems. They seemed to sense instinctively that any help would come from a completely different source if it came at all. In most of these areas nearly all the support available was already coming from churches that had joined together to do what they could.

There is quite a large number of successful projects going on around the country to try to help unemployed people in every age group, and to me the great thing about them is that they can be started by virtually anyone.

In 1981 Peter Raynes, an industrial consultant in Farnham, Surrey, saw his own son and three other teenagers struggling to find jobs after none-too-brilliant examination results. They eventually stumbled on the idea of offering to do 'all the jobs you had always meant to do but never got round to' – mowing the lawn, unblocking drains, putting up shelves – under the inspired title of 'Instant Muscle'.

Seventy jobs came their way in the first week, and Peter was quick to see the potential – not just for them, but for thousands of unemployed young people all round the country. As a business consultant himself, however, he realised how much help they were going to need to turn the idea into something permanent and worth-while.

The way ahead was not easy. He gave up his own job, sold the car and turned the family bungalow into the group's headquarters. For some months it was virtually touch and go, but he started with the basic principle that if you are going to do something then it must be done properly.

Instant Muscle is now operating over seventy cooperatives, and the idea is catching on not only in Europe but as far away as Australia, putting literally thousands of young people to work with interesting creative ventures.

To be successful Instant Muscle needs to be the product of local initiative matched to the needs of the area which, as you would expect, are incredibly varied, from knitting football hats and scarves in the colours of the local team to making ready-packaged sandwiches for firms without canteens, and even running a motor-cycle courier service on the south coast!

When they receive an enquiry from a new area, Instant Muscle usually calls a town meeting of all the voluntary and professional bodies likely to be interested – churches, youth and community services, charities and so on – and then a small feasibility group is set up. As you would expect, with all this professional help and support the failure rate for Instant Muscle groups is very low indeed – only four out of a total of seventy, whereas the national average in the UK is a failure rate of around 40 per cent.

They have found that many companies, in a genuine

effort to help, are very happy to donate warehouses, factory space and vehicles not in use to the co-operatives, often giving more than anyone would have thought likely or possible. It is as if this very action of doing something specific to help unemployed teenagers focuses people's attention on the problem and, incidentally, is something *definite* they can do to help.

Instant Muscle has grown from a management team of two, working from the family bungalow, till they now have over forty people working centrally. Their headquarters are also firmly established in the Rank Xerox offices at Uxbridge, kindly donated free of rent for the purpose. Something about having 'faith as a grain of mustard seed' inevitably springs to mind!

Although this started as a partnership employing other people, the organisers quickly realised that this gave the employees no sense of belonging or of doing their own thing. The whole point, they feel, is to get young people to realise that there are things they can do for themselves, whereas before they simply looked up to the management team as 'bosses', which they found was stifling any initiative.

In a very depressed area of the country another scheme has been in operation since 1971. Known as COMEX (Walsall Christian Council Community Exchange), it unites all possible local and government support in an effort to tackle the problem at every level with 'drop-in centres', youth clubs, training schemes, engineering workshops and community projects. COMEX seems to have thought of almost everything possible. It even includes a Caribbean steel band sponsored by the local brewery!

Young people are able to get training and help in many different fields, from plastering and bricklaying to engineering and catering or to clerical and printing work. Disused halls and warehouses are cannibalised for clubrooms and drop-in centres for out-of-work people. When I visited Walsall they were currently looking for an old building on which the young people could practise their plastering and bricklaying.

Projects like this are operating in many of the depressed areas of the country, but there is still a long way to go and at the moment we are only scratching the surface of the problem. Basically what we need are a few more loaves and fishes and, above all, people who are prepared to say 'Lord, here am I, send me.'

Many of the helpers working with COMEX had themselves been unemployed and, having seen the needs around them, had then stayed on to help. Each was using his own skills to help and to train out-of-work youngsters, and all of them said the same thing – that the work was so rewarding that they would not change to anything else.

In case you know little about the unemployment situation and cannot imagine how you could get together the necessary information and funding even to contemplate such a project in your area, it may help to know that there is government money and know-how available to anyone prepared to help. All the schemes I encountered were using these as a base and expanding from there. Any visit to a local job centre will provide you with the necessary information, from MSC and YOP schemes to job creation and community projects. These not only provide for unemployed people taken on to the schemes, but also for those helping and organising them.

Changing Our Attitudes

Although there has been a lot of talk about helping the unemployed at national level, it has become clear to me that the majority of people who have not been through this experience simply do not want to know about the problem – *even* in our churches.

The clearest illustration of this is still indelibly etched on to my mind. At a diocesan synod meeting, while my husband was still out of work, I listened with considerable interest as one speaker outlined his plans for starting a workshop in the area, which would discuss ways of helping unemployed people. Afterwards I went to talk to him about the project.

His eyes lit up with enthusiasm as I expressed my interest, and he pressed me for ideas of what they could do and who they could get to speak. 'The trouble is that most people round here simply do not want to know,' he said sadly.

If I had any doubts about the truth of this remark they were quickly dispelled. On my way out of the hall I stopped to pick up one or two of the leaflets that he had laid out on the table. Just in front of me a rather large grey-haired lady was being offered a pamphlet.

'*Oh no thank you,*' she said emphatically. '*We don't want to be bothered with all that.*'

I wondered what Jesus would have said in such a situation: 'I was out of work... and you did nothing for me'?

Action Checklist for Those Wanting to Help

Make sure that unemployed people are fully integrated into the life of the church, if possible giving them some definite responsibility and a feeling of genuine involvement.

When you meet them do not continually ask whether there are any jobs coming up. The average time for someone to be out of work is eleven months, which by definition means that for many it will be much longer. Keeping on asking only rubs salt in the wound, and if your friend has the definite prospect of a job you can be quite sure he will tell you!

Don't keep telling these people how many others you know who are out of work. The chances are that they will be only too well aware of this, and it doesn't exactly promote positive thinking!

Get alongside the unemployed as genuine friends, letting them know how much you care without condescension. Remember, it could be you! Encourage them to talk about all the worries they have been carrying single handed – family tensions, lack of money, hopelessness, depression, and so on. Introduce them to friends who might conceivably be able to help or to give them ideas.

Consider whether there is anything you or a group of churches in your area could do to help the unemployment situation. Start a support group; offer church premises for training sessions or drop-in centres; get individuals in the church to take responsibility for an out-of-work family, befriending them and praying for them.

Get together a think-tank of people to see what can be done to help the unemployed in your area. Several heads are always better than one, and one person's ideas can often spark off others. Pursue this line of thought through the local paper, diocesan synods, area charities, etc.

Join with a church in a depressed area and see if it is possible to help in any way – inviting people to your homes, financing their travel, and helping them to find work in a more prosperous area.

Start up a travel fund for local people looking for work, and make sure that it is adequately publicised.

See if there is anything at all that you or your church could do to create new jobs. Start MSC or community schemes, or put to good use the skills of those out of work. Have a look to see what loaves and fishes you possess in your area!

11

Money, Greed and All That

One thought reached my ears over and over again as I talked to people now out of work.

> When I was fully employed I honestly thought of no one but myself. Acquiring more money or possessions seemed perfectly natural to me. But now, looking back, I can't believe how greedy I had allowed myself to become, or how I could possibly have been so blind to all those in need around me.

One assembly-line worker admitted to me that, looking back, he could lay the blame for his own redundancy and that of his fellow workmates fairly and squarely on to the shoulders of corporate union greed.

> They told us we should have more money and we believed them. So we pushed and then we struck and eventually we lost our jobs. We never asked where the money was coming from, or even if we really needed it, but only insisted that *we* should have it at all costs. If only I could have a second chance.

Needless to say, this greed is no special prerogative of union members, but it affects our society through and through – even among those who would call themselves committed Christians. There is a sort of blinkered attitude towards anyone who does not come over our own particular horizon. Their needs are never like ours; their problems are not so pressing; and they can cope while we, apparently, need all that we can get...

If it were possible I should like to transport every complacent, comfortably employed person to spend a few days living alongside the unemployed in some of our inner-city areas just to see at first hand how it feels... and to have to 'sit where they sit'. I am convinced that once they had been there, as everyone who has ever been unemployed can verify, they would never be the same again, and never be able to forget.

It is all too easy to lobby the government or the captains of industry – as indeed we should be doing – about what *they* can do to improve the situation, but what about *us:* are *our consciences* really clear?

The trouble is that, to quote Julian Charley in a recent Church of England Newspaper article, 'Any substantial remedy will involve sacrifice from the rest of us, and it won't be a popular message.'

In East Berlin, for example, people don't know what you are talking about when saying there are not enough jobs available. The streets and the parks there are immaculately swept and kept clean by armies of people put to work on every conceivable task that needs doing, but there is one big difference. This is a totalitarian country where the government has complete power rigidly to keep wages down to a very low level thus making sure that there are jobs for all!

Can you imagine the outcry if that happened anywhere in the consumer societies of the free world!

Voluntarily or forcibly the money has got to come from somewhere and no government has a bottomless supply to handle the problem, *unless* all of us are prepared to make some sacrifice.

There have been many examples in this book already of people who have not just said to their unemployed brethren, 'Go in peace, be warmed and filled' (Jas. 2:16), but have actually gone themselves and *done* something about it.

For example, would it be possible for the church or a group of Christian businessmen living in the area to club together and provide a living wage for a member of the congregation who has been out of work for some time? After all, surely there are plenty of jobs that need doing, and it would be a very real way of showing that we do care enough to act? But there are two factors that must be taken into consideration here. First, the money that is offered must *be* a proper living wage, and second, the job must be something that gives the unemployed person a feeling of self-worth, and not just a charity hand-out!

To offer an unemployed person the sop of a small sum of money to look after the church grounds, or whatever, sounds very thoughtful and well meaning, but how much will it actually help him? Every penny earned will have to be declared against unemployment benefit, and quite frankly a few pounds a month may leave the unemployed person very little better, or even worse off than he was before.

Unfortunately, it has to be said that some Christians can be very niggardly about how much other people should be paid. One man in particular springs to mind. A few years ago he had the initiative to start up his own plumbing business, which in terms of the *amount* of work he was doing went extremely well. However, as he was a Christian the great majority of his clients came from the pews of his home church. One by one almost all of them indicated that 'being a fellow Christian' they expected him to do their work on the cheap – although they were all people in full employment. After six months of this, although he had been almost continually employed, he was making scarcely enough money to pay off his debts, let alone look after his family properly.

In desperation he asked an outsider for help, and was given a booklet listing the standard charges for various jobs. From that moment on he used it in any and every situation except that of genuine need. But I ask you, 'What is wrong with the Christian Church that he even *needed* to take this step?'

One Christian businessman we know long since promised the Lord 50 per cent of his income, and it will be no surprise to learn that his work has increasingly flourished over the years – since God is no man's debtor. People who do not know his secret agreement have often asked how or why it is that James is so successful!

The money has been used almost entirely to put other people to work wherever they are needed, largely on the business side of Christian projects in helping them to become financially viable. If only there were more men like James around . . .

How Much is 'Enough'?

Two years ago old friends of ours returned from many years of teaching in a well-known Christian school in the Himalayas to try to find employment in this country.

I have often found their views interesting and challenging as they look with fresh eyes at the scene here in the West.

After only a few months Alan was offered the headmastership of a large northern school, but nobody could believe that his wife was not going to take up full employment as well. Surely with nearly grown-up children and many years of teaching experience she would want to supplement their income by working as well?

Having lived for years on a low missionary salary in India they were almost overwhelmed by the income that Alan would now be receiving. Barbara was also convinced that her greatest contribution would lie in helping her husband with counselling in and around the school where there were plenty of problems. She had no intention of overstretching herself so that she could not meet these needs.

In addition, they had both noticed with dismay when returning to the UK how many couples had got themselves tied hand and foot to both working flat out just to meet the mortgage payments. There were few enough teaching jobs available, and Barbara honestly felt that it would be only fair and right to allow someone else to earn the salary that she could so easily have had.

A similar story was told me about a couple who lived in an area of heavy unemployment in the Midlands. When her husband, Tim, was out of work for over a year Jennifer started on an administrative job with a very good salary. However, only a few months later Tim had finally been offered the job that he had been after for a long time. Most of their friends thought that this was great. After all they could now pay off their mortgage, and together earn a really tidy sum, starting to enjoy life a bit. They were staggered at Jennifer's response.

Of course she could not keep her job, she said. It would simply not be right when so many others around them had no work at all! Then to their amazement she actually gave in her notice. Perhaps it is worth noting that this couple were not even committed Christians, simply genuinely caring people concerned about the hardship they had seen all around them and putting that concern into action.

Job Sharing

An obvious way for people to show that they genuinely do care is by offering to share the job that they do have with someone out of work – thus spreading the money supply around as well as acquiring more leisure time for themselves.

In general, although the government is now offering a grant to anyone prepared to do this (providing that this will actually bring someone unemployed on to the payroll) the response has been minimal. Incidentally, the grant can also be used if overtime is given up to create a full- or part-time job for an unemployed person.

Two years ago the British Medical Association started a register for any doctor interested in the job-sharing scheme, thinking that here at least they would find a response with so many doctors out of work. Not a single name went down on the list!

Of course it is often said that job splitting is too complicated, too difficult to work out pensions and other contributions and so on. Personally I sometimes wonder if it isn't just that we don't want to part with any of our own personal share of the cake.

Many women have been sharing jobs for a long time, as a means of keeping up with the needs of their home and family, and they have got round these problems well enough. Roger Clarke in his book *Work in Crisis* (St Andrew Press) refers to what he calls these feminist patterns.

> While it has been women workers who have pioneered the increase in part-time working, particularly within the service sector, and it is women who are largely spearheading the experiments with the twinning form of work sharing, it may be that these feminist patterns of a more flexible approach to working hours become the norm for all in the years ahead.

The advances in micro technology and telecommunications are freeing us from the necessity of doing all our work in centralised factories and offices, and opening up the possibility that many workers could now be home based in terms of their employment.

What is within the bounds of possibility is that we could find a place for everybody, whether male or female, young or old, if we based our work expectations more closely on female working patterns.

One of the most successful job-sharing schemes in the UK was started by the personnel director of GEC in Coventry. He recognised that in the lower income brackets it would be difficult to expect a man with heavy family responsibilities to split his income. There would be ample opportunity for younger single folk to do this in the first year of employment, and this was the age group where the need was obviously most pressing.

For the first year two young people divide one job into exactly equal parts, just getting the training and work experience necessary, with the resultant sense of value, while earning marginally more than they would have received on the dole. After this they are entitled to apply for a full-time job with the company.

It sounds to me like the ideal solution to putting a whole lot of young people to work almost overnight – *provided* of course that other youngsters are prepared to share their pay packets.

Perhaps next time that we feel tempted to pass the buck about unemployment by blaming 'them' (the government of the day) for the whole problem, we should try crossing out the word 'they' and replacing this with the first person singular. 'Why don't I do something about the problem?' – and just make sure that we can answer the question with a completely clear conscience.

'Lord when did we see you hungry, naked or in prison? Inasmuch as you did it unto the least of these my brethren you did it unto Me' (Matt. 25:44,45).

12

'Unemployment for the Christian or A Way that You May be Able to Bear It'

Looking back now to the many months that we spent unemployed, I have no idea how we should have coped without our faith behind us. The promise that 'In everything God works for good with those who love him, who are called according to his purpose' (Rom. 8:28) made the biggest single difference to our situation.

Whatever lay ahead we could, in the good times at least, trust that Almighty God knew what He was doing and that He would see us through the tunnel. But this had to be by allowing God to take us through any experiences that He chose to, and by praying that we should learn the lessons that He wanted us to learn and become the richer for this – however unlikely this seemed at the time!

For me this happened in the way that God has always seemed to help me when times are bad, by, quite literally, 'making a way that I might be able to bear it'.

If I look back now I can see that God's forward planning in the situation was quite remarkable. Three or four days before the takeover I was asked to audition for a regular television programme, which was something that I had never done before. Not only the challenge and the interest of the whole project, but also the ongoing fellowship and support of the other people on the programme proved to be a real oasis in the desert that lay ahead.

It was an interest quite outside our home situation, and

a way of sharing with thousands of others the help and support that God was giving us through all the day-to-day problems.

Whenever things got really bad, God seemed to bring me someone else in greater need, or a friend who was a genuine help and support, or some new challenge in my synod or prison work. As each new cloud approached the sun inevitably broke through in the nick of time – but it was certainly never easy.

At the back of my mind all the time was the idea of this book, suggested by an out-of-work Christian friend during the first week of Peter's redundancy.

'Well at least there's one good thing about your being involved in this whole downtime situation, Ann,' he said. 'When it's all over you'll be able to write about it, and get down on paper everything that so badly needs saying.'

Peter's experience was almost identical. Just as the burden of applying for job after job was reaching its height, with the special pain of failing time and again at the final short list (mainly on the grounds of age or lack of UK experience) something new would emerge from the side-lines.

First there was the challenge of fund raising for the Christian youth club premises, helping many deprived London kids who had got themselves into trouble and were on remand or under supervision – a project which needed to raise quarter of a million pounds in just a few months. There was no way that they could have raised the money by themselves, and a combination of prayer and having to go and knock on many different doors in faith, gave Peter a whole new interest, which inevitably stopped him getting too bogged down in his own problems.

Shortly after this someone asked him to help sort out the finances of a small Christian printing firm which had got itself into difficulties. Finally, just as the months looked like stretching on into the future without a break our vicar went off on a six-month sabbatical, leaving Peter, who was senior church warden at the time, to take prime responsibility for all the day-to-day administration of our large and thriving church.

The pattern was fascinating, and clearly worked out by a caring and guiding Mastermind.

What is God Saying to You?

Gradually I became aware of how God was trying to get through to each of the unemployed people we knew, in the pain of their own particular circumstances. Sometimes you had to listen very hard to the still, small voice, but it was there if you wanted to hear it – insistent, unmistakable. And for each one it was different, because we each had a different lesson to learn through our troubles.

The redundancy which hit John so suddenly at the peak of his career very nearly felled him completely, but gradually he realised that being a Christian had inestimable benefits. 'After all,' he asked himself, 'does it really matter if you are Mr Big on one day and Mr Small the next?' Humanly of course it does, as even Christians like status, but hope has always been the grace of God given to us. It is not how far you fall but how you bounce back that is important. *'Above all I think God was teaching me how frail and tenuous the successes of this life really are.'*

John also found that it was his many duties in God's service that kept him going through the time of desolation, and gradually he came to know for certain that God had His hand on him and would see him through.

Andrew had spent eight years in industry when redundancy struck. His basic aims had been to earn more money and to get on in the world. Although his ambition had been to become managing director one day, he knew in his heart that he did not actually admire or respect many of those who held this sort of power. However he was still attracted by the status.

After eighteen months out of work Andrew realised that he had been deceiving himself. He had allowed himself to be carried along by the current and the atmosphere in which he had worked, and what he needed more than anything else was a time to reconsider his values – to stop and think what was really important in life and what God was trying to say to him.

Two things alerted him to the problem. First, he felt a basic unease about the high-powered American salesman who offered him the carrot of a senior position in a few years if he would work for him according to his rules. The more he saw of this man, the more he realised his basic dishonesty with tax evasion and many other shady schemes in which he was involved.

Second, while staying with his parents in a sleepy south-coast town he learnt a very important lesson. The local yacht club included among its members a number of retired captains of industry and political figures, but at the end of their careers. However successful they may have been, he saw that they all came down to the same level, regardless, and those who used their past successes as status symbols were far from happy individuals since basically nobody wanted to know about them.

Retirement was certainly the great leveller, just as he himself had found redundancy to be, and many of those people had spent their lives chasing the wind! That day Andrew learnt the key lesson, that people and relationships mattered more than anything else and, basically, status in itself was unimportant.

Keith had been a positive workaholic – as much out of a

driving sense of duty as for the simple reason that he loved to be fully stretched and occupied.

Every moment of his working life his mind had been full of new ideas for the sales business that he had built up over fifteen years. He had simply loved driving round the country and making new contacts, and even when he was home the work always seemed to come home with him, too.

Not content with this he had even filled his remaining leisure hours to the full, acting as church treasurer, sidesman and house-group leader.

Over and over again his wife, Sarah, had begged him to spend even just a little time with the family and to show some interest in the children. Now in their late teens the family has virtually given up on him. Sarah is fully involved in her new job, the boys have got their own friends and their own interests, and all of them are effectively living their lives 'around' father – although still in the same house.

With devastating suddenness Keith's business has been hit by a downturn in sales due to the recession, and he has been forced to sell out to a rival firm at a considerable loss. Fifteen years of hard work have left him with nothing but bitter memories.

Like John he has realised almost too late how fragile and unimportant such work successes can be, *especially if they are pursued at such a high cost to the family*.

Long ago the family had given up asking Dad to do anything, because he was always too busy. Now that he is kicking around the house all day at a loose end they treat his requests for company and someone to talk to with the contempt they feel they deserve. 'Sorry Dad, we've got homework, you know.'

Sadly he has to acknowledge that the relationship his wife has with the boys has taken time and effort to build, and that he has spent most of his life being 'too busy' for the things that really matter.

At the eleventh hour he was able at least to rescue the shreds of his marriage, and put in time and energy where it was most needed – in the home.

But it was interesting to see that no real opportunities for work came up until Keith had sorted out his priorities and taken a good, hard look at what God was *really* expecting him to do, rather than all the things that he himself had taken on because he wanted to.

The small local firm which eventually took him on provided a much less pressurised framework for living, and by this time Keith was much more ready to accept this.

Fred had worked at the local engineering firm, producing parts for the car industry, since he was a lad of 16. He had never known anything else except Monday to Friday in the workshop, on the bench, and finally as works foreman.

For years he had lived in the same area, worked alongside the same people, and been an integral part of 'the firm'. The sudden collapse of the car industry in his area made this firm and many others close down for good, and at the age of 52 there was really nowhere else for him to go. 'At 50 you're on the scrap-heap, and anyway where would I go to start again now?' asked Fred.

But about six months later, having gone through all the inevitable feelings of rejection, anger, and hopelessness, a new door opened in Fred's life which has, quite literally, made 'the Valley of Achor [trouble] a door of hope' (Hos. 2:15).

The vicar in his local church suggested that Fred should go along and help the new parish worker to start a group for unemployed people in the area. The idea did not appeal to Fred at all. He had always been a very private person, keeping himself to himself, and having to get to know all these strangers seemed fairly horrifying. However he had reckoned without the persuasiveness of

UNEMPLOYMENT FOR THE CHRISTIAN

the vicar and, in particular, the warmth and unmistakable concern of the woman who had recently arrived as parish worker.

Only a few months later the change in Fred is almost revolutionary. From a quiet friendless sort of man he has suddenly discovered that many of the faces he has passed on the street every day are actually real flesh and blood people who want to know him and help him, and who need his friendship, too.

Before long he became the recognised leader of the group, organising many of the activities and helping others in his quiet unobtrusive way, and being a real blessing to many people in the area. Today Fred can honestly look back and say that he is *glad* that he was made redundant, because it is only through this that he discovered a whole new quality of life which had previously been completely closed to him.

For Peter the still small voice was different again. Although he had been a Christian for many years, trusting God with material things and with the nuts and bolts of the family's whole future was a very different thing from just talking about this in theory.

He had always liked to have one foot on the ground materially speaking, and had consequently never discovered any of the riches available to God's people when they stepped out in faith. First the takeover and then redundancy itself had shown him very clearly that the securities of this world could not be relied on but, equally, since he had never really had to trust God for very much, he had little or no experience of drawing on a heavenly bank account.

The crunch for Peter came when after nearly eight months of job hunting he began to realise that God wanted him to show that he trusted Him with the future – no strings attached.

Mission England needed someone to get their fund raising moving for the largest Billy Graham project ever undertaken in the summer of the following year. Peter had been nibbling at this idea for some time in talks with Gavin Reid and Tom Houston, but none of them had felt it was right for him to give up his future prospects in such a way.

Now Peter began to realise that it was an issue of trust between him and God. He needed to commit the future wholeheartedly into His hands as an act of faith, abandoning the job search, and living one day at a time. The sense of peace when he had taken this step was obvious for all to see, as he sank all his energy and enthusiasm into the whole Mission England project.

As so often happens, it turned out that there was a ram in the thicket and the trust was going to be stretched a lot farther for both of us. At about 10.30 p.m. only a few days later, while I was in the middle of a telephone conversation, the operator's voice cut across the call.

'I'm sorry to interrupt you, but there is an urgent call from Sydney, Australia, and you've been on the line for rather a long time.'

There was nothing terribly unusual about this, since Peter had worked for many years with people down under, and we had often been plagued with similar calls, usually in the small hours when it is daylight down there. Thinking nothing of it, I called him as usual...

Hardly half a minute into the phone call and his face was a study in horror and disbelief. 'No, no, I'm sorry, but I've already committed myself to something else.' Pause. 'Well I suppose I could *think* about it, but really I am sure the answer will be "no". Well, all right I'll phone you in a few days.'

As he replaced the receiver he looked as if a snake had bitten him.

During the past eight months he had been adamant

about applying only for jobs that were based in the UK, but under pressure from his career consultant he had agreed to just one or two applications that came in a special category.

One of these was the management of a large group of cocoa and coconut plantations in the Pacific Islands to the north of Papua New Guinea. They had come over to the UK to carry out the interviews two months earlier, but having heard nothing he had forgotten about it. Now, suddenly, he was actually being offered the job, and they wanted a decision in two days' time.

When faced with actually having to pack up and work overseas again after so many years, as well as having to move our two younger children into boarding-school, the job offer took on a completely different complexion. Could this really be what God was asking us to do?

During the eight months of unemployment I had come to see that we might well be faced with this in the end, and now I had a deep sense of peace about the move, despite all that we should be leaving behind. It seemed to me, too, altogether too neat a coincidence that God had withheld the job offer until Peter had committed the future into His hands with no strings attached.

Peter, on the other hand, was not nearly so sure about it and agonised over the decision, even asking for an extension to the time limit. One of the many side-effects of unemployment is a corresponding lack of confidence, and after so long out of work he had begun to feel that he was not up to a new challenge, especially when it was so far away and such an unknown quantity.

In the end we talked and prayed about the decision with four different people whose help and direction we had come to trust, and all of them said 'Go'.

At the time a close friend said to me, 'Hold on to that guidance, you may need it when the going gets tough.' They were to prove very prophetic words!

We eventually left England three months later with Peter feeling encouraged but still apprehensive. If we had only known, our troubles were just beginning...

On arrival in Sydney they greeted us with the news that the volcano above the town where we were to live was on red alert and all women and children had just been evacuated. Peter would have to go on by himself to evacuate the office and take control of the situation.

Hardly the ideal beginning to promote trust in a new job. Did we *really* hear you right, Lord?

Eventually, after the situation had reached nationwide panic in the islands, with TV programmes and headlines about our 'killer volcano' across Australia, everything quietened down, returning to its usual sleepy Melanesian rhythm.

Our contract here is only for three years, coming to an end about the time this book is published. But altogether it has been an interesting, a challenging, breakaway from the rat race and time to reassess our values and the future.

At least unemployment holds far fewer fears for us now. We have learnt to find the wells that sustain us and know that we can really leave the future in His hands, however black things seem.

13

A Christian View of Work and the Future

The other day I had the doubtful privilege of talking to an aggressive new-style businessman who was pursuing his way relentlessly up the ladder of success, rejoicing in every situation that gave him an opportunity of furthering this great ego trip!

Discovering that I was more interested in caring for people, he fired at me a suitable test question. 'How do *you* measure success, then?' he demanded.

I was halfway through a sentence about motivating people to find their full potential when he scornfully cut me short.

'The *only* way to measure success is by the ability to *deliver* profits on the bottom line, that's what counts.'

In a strictly business sense I suppose he was right, but it was his attitude to people as totally dispensable, or grist for the mill of his own success, that sickened me. Wherever he went he was actually *proud* of the fact that he had sacked people out of hand for the single-minded benefit of that all-important 'bottom line'.

Another man I met about the same time was equally successful, but considerably less vocal on the subject. I was aware in talking to him that he *cared* about people, so that to him they were not just statistics on a balance-sheet. I knew that he had also had to make people redundant, but instinctively I saw that this would have hurt him deeply and that he would have given them all the help he could. It was no surprise to me when he talked of his involvement in the local church...

Inevitably in the current work situation there has to be a great gulf fixed between Christian values and those of the world around us.

People Matter More than Things

Living and working in the East as we have done makes it difficult for us not to question some of the contemporary ideas about work and society that many of us have happily accepted as compatible with Christianity.

Japan has been a byword in the Western world for its industrial and business success, but a closer look at Japanese methods gives us a very different picture from the cut-throat individual capitalism of the Western world.

Once someone is taken on to the payroll of a company he becomes in every sense a member of that business family, probably for the rest of his working life. He will be asked to work very hard and to give total loyalty as an employee, but he will be *looked after* accordingly.

Throughout Africa and India there is a widespread concept of the voluntary sharing of wealth and possessions among the family and sometimes even the tribe or village.

Within the Hindu undivided family it is the duty of every individual to support those less fortunate than himself. Even in Papua New Guinea, which we choose to regard as one of the most primitive societies, each individual is obliged by tradition to look after his 'one talks' or cousin brothers in the widest possible sense.

It seems to be glaringly obvious that the Bible expects us to extend this care of *people* and those less fortunate than ourselves as a basic part of our Christian life on earth (Exod. 22:21; Amos 6:3-6).

The following statement from the BSR Report on 'Unemployment and the Future of Work' seems to sum up the situation:

> Some people look critically on... laissez faire capitalism with its emphasis on individualism, competition, the laws of supply and demand in an unfettered marketplace, and the pursuit of self-interest as a means of providing for the good of the community as a whole. They see this as, in effect, a way of structuring the denial of a due concern for the corporate nature of work and of human interdependence in community. They find other philosophies with a greater emphasis on sharing, belonging, equality and fraternity more in keeping with a Christian perspective.

If you think about it many of our current Western ideas about work and the value of what we do are highly questionable in a biblical context. There seem to me to be four basic misunderstandings on the subject, which are not only unChristian, but also greatly increase the burdens of the unemployed person.

'Real Work is Only Paid Work, in a Set Place at a Set Time'

Every wife and mother knows the bitter taste of this particular pill, which is now of course rebounding on to the unemployed as well. However hard one may work at other worth-while things it 'is not the same as a proper job'...

There is no question says Paul Ballard in *Towards a Contemporary Theology of Work* that

> Caring for a home and children is hard and exhausting

work. Not to be able to claim to be socially responsible and economically active while domestically engaged (whatever the gender of the person) demonstrates the artificiality of the modern notion of work as that which is done in a specific place and at a set time.

As Alvin Toffler rightly asks: 'What is the real meaning of employment? Is a laid-off automobile worker who puts a new roof on his home or overhauls his car "unemployed" in the same sense as one who sits idly at home watching the football on TV?'

Surely the fact that God put man on to the earth 'to till it and keep it' (Gen. 2:15) indicates that work is an all-encompassing activity which will overlap into many different areas of responsibility, in the home, in the field and beyond the front door.

'The Value of a Person is Shown by the Work that He Does'

As I stated earlier even many Christians have taken on board the idea that work measures status, or alternatively that without work they are nothing.

This concept that the work that I do is more important than who I am is surely undermined once and for all by the fact that Jesus the Son of God, spent most of His life on earth working at a carpenter's bench.

As Pope John Paul II has pointed out, 'This circumstance contributes in itself the most eloquent gospel of work, showing that the basis for determining the value of human worth is *not primarily the kind of work being done*, but the fact that the one who is doing it is a person.'

Work is a Virtue and Idleness is a Sin

The primary cause of this attitude can be found in God's pronouncement to Adam after he had eaten of the forbidden fruit, and been driven out of the garden.

> Cursed is the ground because of you, through painful toil you will eat of it all the days of your life. It will produce thorns and thistles for you, and you will eat the plants of the field. By the sweat of your brow you will eat your food until you return to the ground (Gen. 3:17-19 NIV).

The necessity for work is part of man's fallen state, and from this stems a lot of our negative thinking on the subject. For example, 'if a man is wealthy and does not need to work then something must be wrong', or, alternatively, 'if he is poor or unemployed it must be because he is trying to avoid the hard work that he should be doing'.

This attitude, says the BSR paper 'Work and the Theologians', can be detected in our thoughts about work today.

> There is a widespread disapproval of people who are dependent on social security benefits. People fear being made redundant. They speak disparagingly of the idle rich. All these situations are felt to be somehow 'wrong' for they challenge the fundamental idea that man *ought* to work. It is a punishment that he cannot or should not seek to escape.

Surely a much more positive and constructive attitude would be to say that now that man's creative use of science and technology has made much of the drudgery of work obsolete and unnecessary, we have been set free to put our time to better use in a hundred different ways.

Work as the Only Means of Belonging in the Community

The destruction of the village and the increased mobility of society in search of work (first started by the Industrial Revolution) has meant that many of us now live our lives in little boxes miles away from family and friends, travelling individually to our places of work. Many have no other natural means of getting to know people than through the props provided by their everyday work.

For most people today work is the primary agent for giving us a sense of belonging in the community, because most work is by nature corporate. To quote William Temple, 'The worst evil of unemployment is its creating in the unemployed a sense that they have fallen out of the common life.'

This corporate activity, says the BSR report, 'is vital for our psychological and spiritual health. We are persons not so much by virtue of being separate individuals as of being persons in the community. We are who we are very much as a result of our relationship with others.'

But as I have shown many times in this book this particular evil of unemployment is the easiest of all to correct once we recognise it for what it is and take steps to deal with the problem.

For Christians the commands of Jesus to love one another and to bear each other's burdens must take on a much wider reality than just meeting outside church on a Sunday.

What Future Work?

Sitting in the unemployment centres and listening to

desperate teenagers almost permanently on the dole in some of our inner cities, I found it was difficult to escape the feeling that some of these young people might never again find themselves in full employment – at least not in the way that we have known this in the past.

The immediate temptation is to think of all the changes taking place as a monster army of robots and technological inventions removing the right to work from under people's noses. And there is no point in disguising that; in a way this *is* what is happening. To quote from a General Synod working paper, *Work and the Future*:

> Electronic checkouts in supermarkets can now be automatically linked to stock control and the reordering of goods from warehouses. Electrically controlled tractors can plough fields without the need for a farmworker in the cab. Fiat have two factories assembling cars using fully automated robots, and a whole car can be welded together in one minute.

Obviously the nature of many jobs has been and will be completely changed by the introduction of such technology – threatening people with these skills. But if we are honest we shall admit that 'many of these jobs were dirty, noisy, dangerous and soul destroying ones which people would be much better off without.'

It is clear that we are in the middle of a completely different kind of social revolution on a world-wide scale, which cannot really be stopped by any political party however well meaning.

Alvin Toffler describes this revolution now taking place in his book, *Third Wave*. After the agricultural revolution the 'second wave' was the rise of industry lasting from the seventeenth century until the present day. But this 'petroholic era', as he calls it, is now 'screeching to a halt'. We are entering the third-wave generation that will combine the use of high technology with decentralisation (reversing the trend of the Industrial Revolution) – a demassed society in which the distinction between work, the consumer and the producer is rapidly being eroded, and a new creature knows as the 'prosumer' will emerge.

The increase in computer technology will make it more and more possible for small industries to be run (like electronic cottages) from the home – in other words returning to a computerised version of the cottage industries that existed before the Industrial Revolution.

There are signs, he says, that this kind of prosumer world is already arriving, in the do-it-yourself shops and self-serve petrol stations. The extension of this idea by electronic means will make all the old distinctions between work and leisure fall apart so that whole new life styles will become a practical possibility. People will find themselves spending their time on production part for exchange and part for their own use.

Again Professor Tom Storrie of Bedford University has come up with the following prediction. 'In about 25 years' time it will take no more than 10% of the labour force to supply society with all its material needs.' He is *not* predicting 90 per cent unemployment, but merely a massive change in the nature of work that people do. The most important input is information, knowledge, know-how and expertise.

The other massive area of growth which is already becoming apparent is the whole range of leisure industries. The *Leisure Shock*, by Chris Jenkins and Barrie Sherman, tells us what to expect in the society of the future.

> Leisure has become the time when money is spent which keeps the economy working. Transport, TV, radio and all its relations, books, newspapers, magazines, eating and drinking out of the house, music, gardening, do-it-yourself – all these and far more besides

will be used as a part of leisure as the working week declines.

They maintain, like Toffler, that as this trend continues so the distinctions between work and leisure will be obliterated. It will become more appropriate to speak of useful activity than of work or leisure as such.

At every level of society it seems that we are in for a big rethink, and one in which Christians can take the lead through sharing and looking for ways that will help us to cope with all these new developments.

Surely *anyone* can be given *some* work to do for his friends and neighbours, whether that work involves mowing the grass, doing the accounts, cleaning out the drains or typing at home? If we can only get away from the stratified industrial full-time concept of a job, then the possibilities are endless. All our traditional ways of thinking about work and leisure, about going out to work and working for yourself, and about the difference between paid and voluntary work will be put into the melting-pot – but we shall have to find practical ways of spreading the money supply around. It is here more than anywhere that the reality of our care and concern for those less fortunate than ourselves will be put to the acid test.

Material for Further Study

Action on Unemployment:
Church Action with the Unemployed, a directory of 100 projects operating round the UK. Video also available. Discussion material and regular up to date information is sent to individuals and churches wishing to become involved.
How to Make a Habit of Success, Bernard Haldane (Warner Books).
Third Wave, Alvin Toffler.
Towards a Contemporary Theology of Work, Paul Ballard (University College, Cardiff).
Unemployment and the Future of Work (Church of England Board for Social Responsibility, Church House, Deans Yard, Westminster SW1P 3NZ).
The Unemployment Handbook, Guy Dauncey (National Extension College, 18 Brooklands Avenue, Cambridge CB2 2HN).
World Out of Work, Giles Merritt (Collins).
The Leisure Shock, Chris Jenkins and Barrie Sherman.

Sources of Direct Help

Details of most projects operating round the country can be obtained from Church Action with the Unemployed, 146 Queen Victoria St, London EC4V 4BY.

Your local Job Centre will give you details of groups for unemployed people operating in your area.

Further Hodder Christian Paperbacks to inform, entertain and deepen your faith.

Free to be Myself

Ann Warren

While the world searches for identity, Christians are supposed to have found it. God promises abundant life and freedom in his service, yet many Christians are struggling under burdens of hopelessness and self-doubt. What has gone wrong?

All too often, writes Ann Warren, Christians accept the world's yardstick for how much they matter as human beings. Drawing from her personal and counselling experience, Ann Warren shows how the blocks of past hurts and present fears can be cleared, opening the way to personal fulfilment and effective witness.

'A beautifully written book which will appeal to all of us who struggle at times with our identity as loving and hopeful Christians.' *Christian Family*

Out of the Ark

Rosalind Allen

A tragedy in the family brought Rosalind Allen to a new awareness of other people's needs – and to an exciting venture of faith.

Starting with a dream – of an outlet for Christian books in the High Street of Stamford, Lincolnshire – reality soon sets in the shape of The Ark, a one-time library van selling Christian books. As other people catch the vision, the ministry develops with the addition of a shop and a coffee bar, and now books are being taken all round the country in a fleet of Good News Vans.

There is hard work and anguish, delight and celebration along the way, and the most effective way of tackling obstacles proves to be prayer. *Out of the Ark* is the story of what God can do in the lives of ordinary people, and of the special ministry of Christian books in enabling personal needs to be expressed and met.